WHAT TO DO WHEN YOU'RE NEW

WHAT TO DO
WHEN YOU'RE
NEW

HOW TO BE COMFORTABLE, CONFIDENT, *and* SUCCESSFUL IN NEW SITUATIONS

KEITH ROLLAG

AMACOM

AMERICAN MANAGEMENT ASSOCIATION

New York · Atlanta · Brussels · Chicago · Mexico City
San Francisco · Shanghai · Tokyo · Toronto · Washington, D.C.

Bulk discounts available. For details visit: www.amacombooks.org/go/specialsales
Or contact special sales: Phone: 800-250-5308 Email: specialsls@amanet.org
View all the AMACOM titles at: www.amacombooks.org
American Management Association: www.amanet.org

This publication is designed to provide accurate and authoritative information in regard to the subject matter covered. It is sold with the understanding that the publisher is not engaged in rendering legal, accounting, or other professional service. If legal advice or other expert assistance is required, the services of a competent professional person should be sought.

LIBRARY OF CONGRESS CATALOGING-IN-PUBLICATION DATA
Rollag, Keith.
What to do when you're new : how to be confident, comfortable, and successful in new situations / Keith Rollag. -- First Edition.
pages cm
Includes bibliographical references and index.
ISBN 978-0-8144-3489-5 (pbk.) -- ISBN 978-0-8144-3490-1 (ebook) 1. Self-confidence. 2. Interpersonal relations. 3. Success. I. Title.
BF575.S39R65 2015
158.2--dc23   2015011043

© 2016 Keith Rollag.
All rights reserved.
Printed in the United States of America.

This publication may not be reproduced, stored in a retrieval system, or transmitted in whole or in part, in any form or by any means, electronic, mechanical, photocopying, recording, or otherwise, without the prior written permission of AMACOM, a division of American Management Association, 1601 Broadway, New York, NY 10019.

The scanning, uploading, or distribution of this book via the Internet or any other means without the express permission of the publisher is illegal and punishable by law. Please purchase only authorized electronic editions of this work and do not participate in or encourage piracy of copyrighted materials, electronically or otherwise. Your support of the author's rights is appreciated.

About AMA
American Management Association (www.amanet.org) is a world leader in talent development, advancing the skills of individuals to drive business success. Our mission is to support the goals of individuals and organizations through a complete range of products and services, including classroom and virtual seminars, webcasts, webinars, podcasts, conferences, corporate and government solutions, business books and research. AMA's approach to improving performance combines experiential learning—learning through doing—with opportunities for ongoing professional growth at every step of one's career journey.

Printing number

10 9 8 7 6 5 4 3 2

To Annie and David

CONTENTS

ACKNOWLEDGMENTS

Books are rarely a solo act, and I had lots of help and support over the past few years as I plotted, schemed, outlined, wrote, and revised this book. I apologize in advance if I've forgotten anybody.

First and foremost on my grand list of thanks are my wife Kathy Harris and my kids Annie and David Rollag. Kathy was first reader and chief editor on every chapter, primary sounding board for new ideas, and my personal therapist as I battled my inner demons and procrastinating ways to get this book out the door. Annie and David gracefully tolerated my frequent trips to the local coffee shop to write, and rewarded me with lots of hugs upon my return.

My graduate assistant Gena Koufos also suffered through early drafts of every chapter, and provided lots of thoughtful input, as did my mom Lottie Rollag. I also appreciate the general encouragement I got from the morning coffee guys at the Muffin House Café.

Of course, many thanks go to my agent Giles Anderson for helping me conceptualize and pitch my book proposal, and to Ellen Kadin and the fine folks at AMACOM for publishing this book.

I've also had an army of colleagues, friends, and students read and comment on various chapters of this book. Thanks goes to Allan Cohen, Sally

Baron, Tom Bowden, Bruce Bumpus, Caroline Daniels, Sinan Erzurumlu, Danna Greenberg, Jeannie Kahwajy, Thais Khuriyeh, Elaine Landry, Rob Major, Jesse McCain, Wendy Murphy, Chris Olkiewicz, Katy Palfrey, Matt Reis, Vonnie Reis, Tracey Reza, Miguel Rivera, Jessi Rosinski, Doris Rye, Victor Seidel, Jonathan Sims, Meehan Tariq, and Scott Taylor.

Over the years I've conducted many interviews with people about their newcomer experiences, including several specifically done for this book. Special thanks goes to recent interviewees Bonnie Anderson, Mahin Arastu, Dave Bernard, Amit Bhatia, Alex Birch, Arturo Bonilla, Allan Cohen, Michael Collins, Jessica Crowley, Ryan Dillon, Eric Echelmeyer, Shawn Edge, Keith Ehrlich, Joe Ewing, Xiao Feng, Keven Gallagher, Danielle Gorlick, Claire Gorman, Ginnie Hatch, Craig Hirsh, Susan Jancourtz, Kazuki Kawaguchi, Alice Korwan, Terry Laughlin, Karen Levine, Eric Lindley, Scott Marcinkus, Marvin Marcus, Fernando Maturana, Chris McEwen, Natalia Ortiz Mena, Domenic Millen, Nick Morwood, Shane Niebergall, Victor O'Farrill, Chris Olkiewicz, Dante Paredes, Samuel Rabin, Astrid Ramirez-Jacobs, Gary Reid, Cliff Riggs, Dave Riley, Hilda Rodriquez Paez, Rodrigo Rodriquez, Chumacero Rubli, Geoff Sauter, Claire Sheth, Melissa Spinks, Dave Sullivan, Mark Therieau, Valerie Todd, Jennifer Velis, and Jeani Warish.

The earliest research for this book occurred while I was a Ph.D. student at Stanford University. I thank all the Stanford graduates and participants of the Mayfield Fellows Program for their newcomer journaling and interviews, and all the input and support I got from my advisors Steve Barley, Bob Sutton, and Tom Byers.

More recently I also appreciate the newcomer research and interviews I've done with co-conspirators Rob Cross and Sal Parise that helped produce several of the quotes and examples in this book. Finally, I must thank my colleagues at Babson College (and particularly the Management Division) for their general support for me and my research. It's a fantastic school and great place to work.

Part 1

WHY NEW SITUATIONS MAKE US NERVOUS

In this section we'll explore how this book can help you become a more confident, comfortable, and successful newcomer. We'll discuss five key behaviors for newcomer success—introducing yourself, remembering names, asking questions, starting relationships, and performing new things in front of unfamiliar people—and see how they are fundamental activities in almost every new situation. You'll also learn how evolution, culture, and our early childhood experiences predispose us to be nervous in new situations and, more important, how to overcome these anxieties through mindful reflection and practice.

ONE

SUCCESS STARTS WITH BEING NEW

To achieve almost anything in life you have to put yourself into new situations. To have a successful career, you often need to change jobs and join new organizations. You get promoted into new teams. Sometimes you're transferred to unfamiliar cities and countries. Outside of work, you're new every time you go back to school for more education or join a new health club to get in shape. You're often a newcomer every time you take up a new hobby, go on a vacation overseas, or check one more thing off your "bucket list."

In fact, it's nearly impossible to accomplish anything meaningful and important in life without at some point having to meet new people, learn new things, and take on new roles. And as a newcomer, how you think and act in those first few seconds, minutes, hours, and days matters. What you do when you're new often determines whether you will find the success, satisfaction, and happiness that drove you to be a newcomer in the first place.

The goal of this book is to help you become a more successful newcomer—across all kinds of new situations. We'll explore the science of newcomer success and give you a set of strategies, techniques, and exercises to become:

- More productive and confident in your new role
- Better connected to new co-workers, classmates, group members, and neighbors
- Less anxious and awkward around strangers
- More willing to seek out those new experiences that make life interesting, rewarding, and fun

NEWCOMER SUCCESS: FIVE KEY SKILLS

I've been studying newcomer success for over twenty years. In the workplace, I have interviewed hundreds of new employees in a variety of roles, levels, and industries. I have observed newcomers while they work, and have talked to their managers. I've also asked newcomers to keep journals about their first few weeks on the job and have conducted newcomer surveys across many organizations.

Outside of the workplace, I've interviewed newcomers joining schools, churches, neighborhoods, theater groups, health clubs, and even rock bands. I've interviewed college students moving into residence halls, and senior citizens moving into retirement communities. I've talked with people taking classes on everything from swimming, guitar, yoga, and skiing to beekeeping. Through these interviews I've been trying to understand what successful newcomers do that allows them to have such positive, rewarding experiences. How do they get up to speed quickly? How do they integrate themselves into their new group? How do they get the information and advice they need to be productive in their new role?

I've discovered that the secret to newcomer success is no secret at all. It mostly comes down to our willingness and ability to do five key things:

1. Introduce ourselves to strangers.
2. Learn and remember names.
3. Ask questions.
4. Seek out and start new relationships.
5. Perform new things in front of others.

For most of us, these five skills are both the key to newcomer success and our greatest source of anxiety in new situations. For example, although we know that introductions are critical to getting connected, we are reluctant to approach and introduce ourselves to new people. We realize that remembering names creates a great "second" impression, but we discover we're unable to recall names when we meet people again.

We know that asking questions is often the only way to get the information we need, but we hesitate to bother busy, important people. We understand that all work gets done through relationships, but we are reluctant to start and build new ones. Finally, we find ourselves anxious about performing our new role in front of unfamiliar people, even though we know that newcomers are expected to start out slow and make a few mistakes.

The Networking Event that Wasn't

Does any of the following seem familiar?

You know you're supposed to network, and this event is the perfect opportunity to build new connections. But as you walk into the room, you are overwhelmed by the unfamiliar crowd, and you desperately search the sea of strangers for a few friendly faces. Finding some, you go say hi, and spend the rest of the event huddled and chatting with those you already know, never really meeting anyone new.

Or you don't see a friendly face, and nobody approaches you to introduce themselves, so you end up on the sidelines staring at your smartphone. You pretend that you've got urgent email or text messages that you just have to respond to. That way you can justify why you're standing in the corner by yourself for most of the event.

Either way, as you leave, you decide that the meeting wasn't a good networking opportunity after all.

If you've had this experience, you're not alone. Columbia University researchers Paul Ingram and Michael Morris once organized a networking mixer for a group of executives. Over 95 percent of the attendees said that a primary reason for coming to the mixer was to meet and develop relationships with new people. Prior to the event, they asked each executive to identify which people on the invitation list they already knew.

As the executives arrived, each one was given a special electronic nametag, which allowed Ingram and Morris to track the movements and conversations of each executive over the course of the 80-minute event.

They found that, despite the executives' intentions to meet new people, most of them spent the event with people they already knew. They rarely approached and introduced themselves to strangers, and those who did meet new people were introduced by someone familiar to both. What was Ingram and Morris's advice for those looking to meet new people at networking events? Don't bring your friends along.[1]

In other words, the key to sucessful networking often is overcoming your reluctance to approach and introduce yourself to new people—a fundamental newcomer skill. This book can help. In Chapter 5, we'll dissect and analyze the social dynamics surrounding introductions, and we'll explore why it causes so much anxiety. We'll also review specific strategies and exercises to help you:

- Approach strangers with less anxiety
- Confidently introduce yourself

- Make a good first impression
- Engage in small talk that helps establish a positive relationship
- Leave the introduction with permission to approach people later for help, advice, and fun

What's Her Name Again?

While newcomer success often starts with the ability to proactively introduce yourself, how you think and act the second time you meet someone matters, too. Has the following ever happened to you?

> You see her all the time. Maybe it's a co-worker, a classmate, or a mother standing on the sidelines at your kid's soccer game. The first time you met her you exchanged names and had a really nice conversation, and it's clear that she is someone you'd like to know better. But the next time you meet she calls you by name, and you panic because you can't remember hers. You reply with an enthusiastic but somewhat lame greeting like "Hey, how are you doing?" and try to pretend you know her name.
>
> You continue to meet from time to time and have friendly interactions, but you become more and more uncomfortable because you still can't recall her name. Admitting it now would really be awkward. The crazy thing is that you can remember almost everything else about her except her name. Your greatest fear is that someday you'll run into her while you're with another person, and you'll be expected to introduce them to each other.
>
> You'd like to get to know her better, but the whole "name thing" makes you reluctant to take things further. So you stick to quick pleasantries, avoid her when you are with another person, and hope she doesn't notice.

If this sounds familiar, it's hardly unique. Approximately 80 percent of the people I've interviewed say they are bad at remembering names.

Many can point to newcomer situations in which they've been anxious and reluctant to interact with people they've recently met because they can't recall their names.

Most people fear the embarrassment of blanking on someone's name. The British gaming company Ladbrokes conducted a survey of 2,000 people and found that the respondents' number one most embarrassing moment was forgetting the name of someone they were introducing. Their number three most embarrassing moment was getting someone's name wrong.[2]

But there is hope. In Chapter 6 we explore why most of us are bad at recalling names, and what you can do about it. We'll examine the neuroscience of memory and learn why the way we process and store peoples' names can cause problems with recall. We'll also look at the social dynamics of introductions, which often prevent us from even hearing, learning, and memorizing a person's name in the first place. More important, you'll find a variety of techniques you can use before, during, and after introductions that will help you:

- Learn and memorize the names of new people.
- Confidently recall their names when you meet them again.
- Avoid embarrassment when you don't remember a name.

Time Flies and It Seems Too Late

Many people I've interviewed say the newcomer success they care most about is being successful in a new job. Thinking back to the last time you joined a new organization, does any of the following ring a bell?

You're a few weeks into your new position, but you still don't know everyone. Your boss gave you a whirlwind tour the first day, but the introductions were so fast you barely got to know anybody. You'd like to ask certain key people for help and advice, but you're reluctant to approach them. Either you were never introduced to them in the first place or they always seem busy, and you don't want to impose or interrupt their work. Besides, now that several weeks have gone by, you feel you should already know the answers to some of your questions.

You thought by now you'd have made a few new friends at work, but so far it's been mostly minor chit chat with random people. Lunch is still uncomfortable—sometimes you are invited to join the "lunch bunch," but often they leave without you. Looking back, you wish you had asked more questions and worked harder to make new friends, but it seems too late and awkward to do it now.

I've heard variations of this story from dozens of newcomers. Some of the underlying frustration and regret was caused by managers who didn't take the time to properly introduce the newcomers to others in the office. Some of it was caused by co-workers who weren't welcoming and accepting of new people. But some of it was the result of the newcomers' reluctance to ask questions and develop new relationships.

When I've asked newcomers "If you could do it all over again, what would you do differently?" by far the most common answer I've received has been "Ask more questions." In Chapter 7 we'll explore why we're reluctant to ask questions of relative strangers, especially busy, influential people. We'll analyze the social dynamics surrounding question-asking and review several techniques you can use to:

- Be more strategic and proactive in asking questions.
- Approach and ask questions with less anxiety.
- Ask questions in ways that create or maintain a positive impression.

Newcomer success also happens through relationships. We need them to learn new roles, acquire information and advice, be accepted by the new group, and build the influence we need to achieve our goals.

Relationships are also the key to newcomer satisfaction. The Gallup

Organization has conducted thousands of company surveys with millions of employees. They found that one of the strongest predictors of job satisfaction is how strongly an employee agrees with the statement "I have a friend at work."[3]

Though we make friends throughout our lives, only a few people I've interviewed consider themselves extremely good at developing relationships. In Chapter 8, we'll do the following:

- Explore why we're reluctant and awkward about starting new relationships.
- Investigate the science of relationship development (from acquaintances to friendships).
- Discover several strategies that will help you move beyond the initial introduction and develop meaningful relationships.
- Find ways to practice and get better at starting relationships and "fitting in."

The Reluctant Participant

Finally, here's one more situation common to newcomers:

You've walked, driven by, or seen an advertisement for classes or lessons in something you'd really like to learn or do. Maybe it's public speaking, sales strategies, cooking, or aerobics. Maybe it's photography, dance, yoga, or a foreign language. You really want to take the class, but you're reluctant to go.

You know it'll be awkward to meet the instructors and other participants, but you're mostly worried about performing in front of other people, many of whom are probably more experienced and skilled than you are. You'll be embarrassed when they find out what a total beginner you are. You tell yourself you should have started doing this long ago, when you were younger. Instead of taking the class, you stay away, convincing yourself that you really didn't want to learn that skill, sport, or hobby anyway.

This is a common story, and all of them seem to result from the teller's reluctance to be seen by others as an awkward, mistake-making, less-than-perfect newcomer. At work it can keep you from taking on new roles, developing new skills, or presenting your best ideas. Outside of work, it can simply keep you from trying new things—so you lose out on all the good things that come with new experiences.

In Chapter 9, we'll explore the science of newcomer performance to:

- Understand why we are anxious and reluctant to perform in new groups.
- Develop strategies to move from a focus on "being good" to a focus on "getting better."
- See the value and benefits of approaching new situations with a "beginner's mind."

Of course, there are other things you need to do to be a successful newcomer. You need to establish credibility and build trust. You need to negotiate responsibilities and role expectations. You need to attend orientations and training sessions. If you're a new leader, you have to create a shared purpose and generate early wins to create momentum for change.[4]

In this book, I focus on these five newcomer skills because I believe they are the fundamental skills required for newcomer success. The more confident, comfortable, and willing you are to perform these five basic skills, the more successful you can be as new leaders, team members, students, neighbors, volunteers, parishioners, tourists, and any other newcomer role you decide to take on.

Think of these skills as equivalent to catching, throwing, and hitting in baseball, or scoring and passing in soccer. They are the foundational skills that make all other newcomer and new leader success strategies possible. For example, you often can't establish credibility and trust without first introducing yourself. You can't build networks without being able to start and nurture new relationships. You can't hit the ground running without asking questions and learning to perform your new role. And it's hard to get people to follow you if you can't remember their names.

Most managers (and writers of newcomer books) assume you're already good at these five key newcomer skills, and therefore tend to ignore them. They expect that because you've grown up, gone to school, and interacted with hundreds of people over the years, you're already a master at making introductions, remembering names, asking questions, and so on.

My interviews with newcomers tell a different story. Most of us don't consider ourselves exceptionally good, or even good, at these critical behaviors. Our reluctance or lack of confidence in one or more of these skills is often at the heart of why we don't put ourselves out there and create the newcomer success we desire.

Unfortunately, these five newcomer skills also are not things you typically learn in school, or even in training classes at work. Think about it. Have you ever taken a course on making introductions? Been taught how to consistently remember names? Received coaching on how to confidently ask questions? Been taught how to start relationships and make friends? Or "learned how to learn" to perform new roles and tasks?

We value people who can quickly get up to speed, but organizations rarely spend any time actually teaching their employees how to make introductions, remember names, ask questions, develop relationships, or perform new tasks. Usually you have to figure these skills out on your own.

NEWCOMER ANXIETY IS NORMAL

As we will see in Chapter 3, being a little nervous in new situations is completely normal. Much of our anxiety surrounding these five key newcomer skills comes from two sources. First, we're genetically hard-wired to be nervous around strangers. Second, we learn at an early age to fear and avoid unfamiliar people.

From a genetic standpoint, newcomer anxiety is the evolutionary outcome of having distant ancestors who lived in a prehistoric world where meeting strangers was often a rare and dangerous event. It was also a world where getting excluded by one's group and sent out into the wilderness alone was practically a death sentence. As a result, we've evolved to have a natural fear of both strangers and social rejection.

However, our prehistoric brains don't work so well in a modern world where we constantly find ourselves surrounded by unfamiliar people. Scientists estimate that for much of history, humans were new-comers only a few times in their entire life, and probably met or were aware of only a few hundred people. Today we move in and out of new-comer situations all the time, and meet hundreds and perhaps thousands of new people every year. But we still carry our inherited fears into everyday newcomer situations that are significantly less dangerous and life-threatening than they were thousands of years ago.

When we were very young we also learned to be nervous around new people. Some of us observed, copied, and internalized our parents' anxieties and assumptions about strangers. Some of us came to associate the presence of strangers with abandonment, especially when our parents left us with unfamiliar babysitters and daycare providers. Some of us probably had some less-than-positive early experiences meeting new kids and adults that reinforced our natural fear of strangers.

But most of us were also taught to fear and avoid unknown people. From an early age we're told "Don't talk to strangers." Many are taught to yell "No!" and run away from unfamiliar adults, especially those who approach us when we're alone or without "safe" adults present.

However, when we grow up and become adults ourselves we're suddenly encouraged to put ourselves out there, meet new people, and try new things. Ironically, this requires us to approach and interact with the same kinds of adult strangers we were supposed to avoid our entire childhood.

GETTING BETTER THROUGH REFLECTION AND PRACTICE

Despite what nature and nurture has taught us, we can overcome our anxieties and become more confident, comfortable, and successful newcomers, but it takes reflection and practice. In Chapter 4, we'll learn that one way to do this is to recalibrate our prehistoric brains by reflecting upon our fears and anxieties in new situations and compare what we worry might happen with what actually does happen. Throughout this book I provide exercises and thought-provoking questions to help you stop overestimating social risk and become more comfortable introducing yourselves, asking questions, and so on.

The other way to reduce our anxiety and reluctance is to improve our performance, and that only happens through deliberate, mindful practice. Have you ever wondered why over the course of our lives we can introduce ourselves to thousands of people, remember hundreds of names, ask countless questions, make tons of friends, and yet still be awkward and reluctant each time we perform these basic newcomer skills? The reason is that we mostly do these things mindlessly and never take the time to pay careful attention to our performance, figure out how we can improve, and experiment with new approaches.

For each of the five newcomer skills, I provide a set of techniques and exercises to help you deliberately, mindfully analyze and improve your performance through practice. Most of these techniques, exercises, and games can be added to your regular daily routine. Because you see and interact with strangers almost every day, you'll find countless opportunities to practice, observe, and refine your skills. Many of these opportunities offer you a relatively safe and low-risk way to practice, so you can become confident and better prepared for the newcomer situations you most care about. All it takes is a sincere, personal commitment to improve.

HOW TO GET THE MOST FROM THIS BOOK

After this introductory chapter, in Chapter 2 we'll see how frequently we move in and out of newcomer situations and understand why getting better at being new can be such a benefit. In Chapter 3 we'll examine how evolution and social learning has set us up to be nervous in new situations; and in Chapter 4, you'll see how self-reflection and practice are the keys to getting better at the five newcomer skills.

Then, over the next five chapters, we will systematically focus on each of the newcomer skills:

1. Introducing yourself (Chapter 5)
2. Remembering names (Chapter 6)
3. Asking questions (Chapter 7)
4. Starting new relationships (Chapter 8)
5. Performing in new situations (Chapter 9)

In each chapter, we'll examine:

- Why the skill is important to your success
- Why it causes so much stress and anxiety
- How to get better and more comfortable doing it
- How to find or create opportunities to practice

I suggest that you first read through each skills chapter to get the big picture. Then, ask yourself whether you find that specific skill a challenge or a major source of anxiety when you find yourself in new situations. Over the next few days, mindfully observe and reflect upon both your performance and the associated emotions you experience in new situations. Based on what you discover, you may decide to tackle a particular skill first. Or, you might decide to start with the chapter and skill that you:

- Think will give you the biggest "bang for the buck" in terms of overall improvement.
- Feel the most comfortable thinking about and practicing right away.
- See the most opportunities for practice in the next few weeks.

Of course, you may decide to tackle them in the order presented. It doesn't really matter where you begin.

Finally, in Chapter 10, we will explore ways to "give back" and help others become more successful newcomers. We'll round out the book in Chapter 11 with some final words of advice and a few success stories to motivate you to "get out there" and become a better, more confident newcomer.

In addition, please check out the book website at www.whenyoure-new.com for more newcomer resources and practice tips.

———

Ultimately, the key to becoming a better newcomer is to stop seeing "being new" as something you fear and endure, but as an interesting challenge you can learn to improve through reflection and practice.

TWO

ALWAYS A NEWCOMER

Over the course of your life you will likely find yourself in newcomer situations thousands of times. And in almost every new situation you will have to introduce yourself, remember names, ask questions, start relationships (no matter how temporary), and perform new things in front of people you don't know.

A little bit of anxiety about doing these things is actually a good thing. When you're nervous your brain releases a tiny bit of adrenaline that flows through your body and helps keep you focused and alert. But too much anxiety can cause you to:

- Perform poorly.
- Not enjoy the experience.
- Avoid subsequent new situations.

If you feel that you're more anxious in new situations than you want, do you really wish to experience that excessive nervousness thousands of more times in your life?

WE ALL START AS NEWCOMERS

If you think about it, the first thing we ever do as a member of the human race is be the newcomer. As soon as we get pushed and pulled down that long tube and emerge into the light, we're surrounded by strangers. First, we're new to our family and begin life-long relationships with our parents and siblings. Soon, we're newcomers at daycare facilities, pediatrician's offices, and playgrounds, as well as to family, friends, relatives, and other children—in fact, wherever our parents take us.

Lessons from Childhood

Eventually, we enter elementary school, and for the next twelve years we progress through an endless series of new classrooms, new classmates, and new teachers, as well as new after-school and outside activities, teams, bands, theater groups, clubs, summer camps, and scout troops.[1] We also may take on part-time jobs where we are confronted with co-workers and tasks that are new to us.

Through all these early experiences we start building our ability and confidence in the five newcomer skills. Of course, there are precocious four-year-olds who boldly and confidently introduce themselves to everyone—neighborhood kids, teachers, doctors, parking lot attendants, even the homeless. But for most of us, learning to introduce ourselves starts out as a relatively stressful experience, and we never completely lose our awkwardness each time we do it. Still, we quickly discover that introducing ourselves is a critical first step toward making friends and being accepted by new groups. How we come to terms with introducing ourselves as children shapes how we think and feel about introducing ourselves for the rest of our lives.

The same thing goes for all the other newcomer skills. When we're young, we can blissfully interact without caring whether we remember other kids' names, but it becomes increasingly embarrassing to forget a name as we get older. From pre-school onward, we're taught how to ask questions (raise your hand!), but we soon discover this strategy isn't really appropriate outside the classroom. We never take a class on making friends, but through trial and error we reach varying degrees of comfort and confidence in starting relationships with kids our own age.

Finally, school is all about having to perform new, potentially embarrassing things—music and art classes, spelling bees, and those ubiquitous front-of-the-class book reports—before unfamiliar teachers and classmates. But all of these pale in comparison to the times we're forced to dress up as a flower, a letter, or historical figure, herded on stage in front of strange grownups, and then made to sing or say something cute while the parent paparazzi blind us with camera flashes. None of this would ever cause us to become nervous in new situations, would it?

Lessons from Adolescence

Once we hit puberty and discover romance and sexual attraction, "newcomer" takes on a whole new meaning and level of risk. We struggle to ask intelligent questions on dates, and we fear saying the wrong thing. And, of course, high school comes with its own set of newcomer problems: new students to meet, new teachers, new subjects, and new activities.

Lessons from Young Adulthood

If we head off to college, we face new professors, classmates, and dorm mates, as well as fraternities, sororities, sports teams, and student clubs. We may study and travel abroad, take summer jobs, or intern in new organizations. By the time we graduate from college we've experienced hundreds, if not thousands, of newcomer situations; and once we take our first full-time job, we're destined for thousands more.

THE BIG CHALLENGE: NEW AT WORK

If you are a typical American worker, you will be a newcomer to at least eleven different organizations by the time you are forty-eight years old, and several more before you retire.[2] We're often new with every restructuring, merger, acquisition, and downsizing. In fact, it's safe to say that even if we don't change jobs, we will likely be new dozens of times over the course of our work career. And this doesn't even include all the committees, task forces, and other ad hoc work groups we might participate in, or events like internal conferences, training programs, and company parties that temporarily put us in new social situations. Each time we're new we have to introduce ourselves to co-workers, remember names, ask questions, start relationships, and perform our new group role in front of relative strangers.

New to Customers, Clients, and Suppliers

But that's not all. If you're currently working, how many times in the past few months have you visited a new customer, client, supplier, or governmental agency? Consultants and independent contractors are often moving in and out of new client organizations every few months. Travelling salespeople are making visits to new or potential customers every week. Commercial plumbers, electricians, and others in the "trades" are often temporary newcomers to workplaces every day.

Now granted, these kinds of newcomer situations have a very different feel and significance compared to joining a new company. We're not starting a new job, or getting a new boss, or settling into a new cubicle. But in each of these situations we still have to make introductions, remember names, ask questions, start relationships (even if very temporary), and do our job in front of new people. More importantly, how well we perform when we're new in these situations often has a huge impact on our overall performance. Could we ever make a sale, please a client, or secure a new supplier without performing these five newcomer skills?

Being New and the All-Important Job Search

Finally, in between all of your jobs you are a newcomer every time you attend networking events and career fairs, as well as every time you interview for a new job. Who usually gets hired? The candidates who can:

1. Confidently introduce themselves and remember the names of recruiters, interviewers, and potential co-workers.
2. Ask thoughtful questions.
3. Establish rapport and build positive relationships with everyone they meet.
4. Demonstrate in interviews and skill tests that they can perform the job.

I hope it's clear by now that regardless of what you do at work you will likely find yourself new all the time, and how well (and confidently) you perform as a newcomer has a big impact on your ultimate performance and job satisfaction.

SOCIAL CHALLENGES: NEW PEOPLE, NEW PLACES, NEW EXPERIENCES

The Census Bureau estimates that the average person in the United States moves every four years, and can expect to move over eleven times during his or her lifetime.[3] Every time we move we are newcomers to neighborhoods, apartment buildings, and condo associations. We join new churches, health clubs, and civic organizations, and send our kids to new schools. We seek out and are new to grocery stores, restaurants, dry cleaners, and every other store and service we use in our busy lives. We have to find and build relationships with new doctors, dentists, landscapers, and plumbers.

The simple act of moving generates dozens of newcomer situations. If you don't introduce yourself to your new neighbors in the first few days or weeks, it becomes increasingly awkward to do it later. You're flooded with new names and struggle to keep them all straight. You have to ask lots of questions to reestablish access to all the daily goods and services you took for granted. And while you've performed all these daily life activities at your previous locations, every new encounter holds the potential for embarrassment if you unknowingly break the rules and perform differently from the "natives" around you.

Relationships with spouses and partners trigger a whole new set of newcomer experiences. Regardless of whether you get married or not, you become a newcomer to someone else's parents, siblings, and step-families, as well as to their extended network of uncles, aunts, and cousins. Your ability to be a good newcomer with the "in-laws" can pay huge dividends. And if things don't work out and you end up in another relationship, you're new all over again.

If you become a parent, you're new to obstetricians, birthing classes, baby stores, and delivery rooms. Then you're also new to pediatricians, daycare centers, playgrounds, schools, and parent-teacher organizations. You become a spectator to an endless parade of games, practices, recitals, and programs. Through your child's activities you meet and start new relationships with other parents and families, and your network of friends quickly shifts from the mostly-single to the mostly-married-with-kids. The more children you have, the more newcomer situations you'll find yourself in. Once again, all these newcomer skills come into play as you become a connected, informed, and engaged parent.

According to Pew Internet Research, 75 percent of all adult Americans are active members in groups outside of work, and the average person spends more than six hours a week across an average of 3.5 organizations.[4] Approximately 40 percent of us are involved in churches or other religious organizations, and the rest of our participation is spread across groups such as sports and recreation leagues, charitable and volunteer organizations, community groups, neighborhood associations, support groups and political parties.[5] As our interests, opportunities, and locations change, we move in and out of dozens of these outside groups. With each one our newcomer skills help determine how well we become an integrated, engaged member, and how much satisfaction and fun we get out of the groups' activities.

New hobbies and pursuits are another source of newcomer experiences. If we take classes, we're new to instructors and our fellow students. Hobbies like painting, gardening, quilting, and photography all have their own social world of enthusiasts and a bewildering set of new technologies and techniques.

Sports also have their rules, equipment, techniques, and learning paths from beginner to expert. For example, if we decide to learn how to ski, we are typically new to ski resorts, rental shops, ski classes, ski lifts, and other skiers. How we think and act as a newcomer in these situations matter. Sadly, the National Ski Areas Association estimates that over 85 percent of all first-time skiers never return, and I suspect for many it's because the anxiety that came with being a new skier overwhelmed any fun they got from being on the slopes.[6]

Vacation and travel is also a time when we find ourselves newcomers in a variety of ways. Travelling itself can make us new to unfamiliar cities, roads, and transit systems, and make us newcomers to temporary groups of fellow passengers and tourists. And once again the five newcomer skills come into play. For example, if you go on a cruise for the first time, you will likely introduce yourself to a few of the passengers and cruise staff, and there will be some limited social expectation that you'll remember the names of those people you interact with most frequently. You'll likely have many questions about where to go and what to do during the cruise. Though you might avoid lots of socializing on the ship, most people on cruises do enjoy getting to know a few passengers or staff members during their stay. Finally, there are routines like port calls and buffet lines that one must learn and perform. While taking a cruise may not have the high stakes associated with being new at work, there are still plenty of situations associated with the five skills that can cause anxiety and discomfort.

GET BETTER NOW, AVOID REGRETS LATER

Like it or not, the fact is that for the rest of your life you'll be moving in and out of countless newcomer situations. Some will be temporary and relatively inconsequential, like joining strangers in an elevator or standing in line at a new deli. Some will involve familiar tasks but unfamiliar people, such as eating at a McDonald's in an unfamiliar city. Other situations will involve familiar people but unfamiliar activities, such as joining your family on a river-rafting trip.

Granted, you usually do not need to perform all five newcomer skills in every new situation. In an unfamiliar store, you may need to introduce yourself to sales clerks and ask questions, but there may be little expectation you'll remember their names or build much of a relationship with the cashier.

At a sporting event or orchestra concert you may be surrounded by strangers, but there is little expectation that you will introduce yourself or remember their names if you do. Still, you may need to ask a few questions, and there is still an expectation that you will perform the role of fan or concert goer in an acceptable way.

Think about the newcomer experiences you've had in the past few months. How many times did you introduce yourself to a stranger? Try to memorize or recall a name? Ask a stranger a question? Strike up a conversation with someone you had just met? Try to perform something new?

As I've said before, none of these newcomer skills are things we typically learn in school, or are emphasized in training classes at work. We value people who can quickly get up to speed, but organizations rarely spend any time actually teaching people how to make introductions, remember names, ask questions, develop relationships, and learn how to perform new things. Usually we have to figure these out on our own. But hopefully it's now clear that making a commitment to improve the five skills discussed in this book can make all your future newcomer situations more productive and less stressful.

Over the course of our lives we all accumulate regrets. Some are for things we did, but often we regret things we didn't do, such as opportunities we didn't pursue or relationships we never developed. When these moments of choice come along, how many do you let pass by because you feel awkward introducing yourself to strangers, asking questions, starting up relationships, or admitting that you are a beginner? More important, how many of those regrets do you want to continue accumulating?

The good news is that many of these future newcomer situations (both the ones you suddenly find yourself in and the ones you proactively seek out) provide ideal opportunities to practice and improve your ability to perform in front of strangers. In some of these situations, especially those with long-term consequences like new jobs, schools, and organizations, you'll really care about performing well. In other, less consequential temporary situations, you'll likely never see the people again, and you can practice the skills you will learn from this book, knowing that any mistakes and failures will have little impact beyond the embarrassment of the moment.

But before we dive into the five newcomer skills and learn how to get better and more comfortable with each of them, we first need to understand why new situations cause us so much anxiety. Read on . . .

THREE

NATURE AND NURTURE
The Science of Newcomer Anxiety

In this chapter we will explore why new situations often make us nervous and uncomfortable. In particular, we'll examine:

- How humans evolved to be anxious around strangers
- How children learn to fear and avoid unfamiliar people
- Why these anxieties are often counterproductive in today's world, where interacting with strangers is commonplace and rarely dangerous

Ultimately, my goal in this chapter is to convince you that being a *little* anxious in new situations is normal and helpful (in future chapters we'll figure out what to do about excessive anxiety.)

COGNITIVE DISSONANCE: OUR EXPERIENCE
VERSUS OUR FEAR OF THE NEW

We spend our entire lives being new. Every time we change jobs, move to new neighborhoods, take new classes, or join new clubs, we find ourselves surrounded by strangers and unfamiliar social situations. Most of us have had hundreds or thousands of these newcomer experiences in our lifetime, and thousands more to go. According to the people I've interviewed, the vast majority of these newcomer experiences go well. Occasionally we might truly embarrass ourselves, or find ourselves snubbed by strangers. Once or twice in our lives we might find ourselves in real danger. But most of the time we have a relatively good newcomer experience. Sometimes these experiences are incredible and even life-changing. Often they are uneventful, even forgettable. Usually they go reasonably well, and we rarely regret putting ourselves into new situations.

With all these mostly positive experiences, you would think that we would already have learned to be comfortable and confident in new situations. Instead, most people I've interviewed still feel some level of anxiety when they're new, even in those situations where past experience would suggest there is *little reason* for being nervous.

Why is there a disconnect between what we've experienced in past newcomer situations and what we fear will happen in the next one? More specifically, why are we still reluctant to:

- Approach and introduce ourselves to unfamiliar people, when almost everyone we've met in our lives has greeted us warmly?
- Ask a stranger a question, when most people we've approached have been happy to help us out?
- Perform new things in front of new people, when our performance (and other's reactions to it) almost always goes much better than we think it will?

Many people I've interviewed have wondered why they continue to be anxious in new situations. For example, one MBA student described her reluctance to approach and introduce herself to strangers:

> "When I don't know someone it's really hard for me to approach them and start asking questions. I usually wait until they start to ask me questions."

When I asked what she was afraid of, she said:

> "I really don't know. I've asked the same thing of myself. I'm extremely uncomfortable to take that first step and talk to someone, and when I do I keep replaying the conversation in my head and always find something I said that was wrong."

HOW BEING NEW AFFECTS CREATIVITY

Not only do we seem to automatically become anxious in new situations, but researchers have found that just the thought of being new makes us nervous. Social psychologist Richard Moreland and his colleagues demonstrated this in a clever experiment. They put together groups of five strangers. Before the groups met for the first time, the researchers randomly lied to two of the five people in each group, telling them that the rest of the group had been meeting for several weeks, and they were the newcomers in the group.

Just the simple act of telling these two people they were new changed their outlook. They were much more nervous about the upcoming meeting and less confident about their ability to contribute to the group (compared to the other three people in the group who assumed they *all* were new.[1])

Other researchers have found that when we actually join a group and start interacting, being new can also affect our performance. Anthropologists Dennison Nash and Alvin Wolfe put groups of four strangers together and had them brainstorm creative interpretations of Rorschach-like inkblot pictures. After a few minutes and a few pictures, they randomly transferred one person in each group to another group. Even though everyone had the *same* amount of experience interpreting inkblots, the people who were transferred to a new group suddenly started making fewer creative interpretations. After a several minutes, the researchers returned the individuals back to their original groups, and their creative output went back to normal.[2]

In other words, there was something about being new to a group that inhibited an individual's creativity and performance. Even for something as simple as interpreting inkblots, and when everyone in the group had the same amount of experience with the task. And even when newcomers knew they were joining a group that had been formed *only a few minutes earlier*.

Why do we automatically get anxious in new situations, even when our past experience suggests there is little reason to do so? Why does just the *thought* of being the newcomer cause us to be less comfortable and confident in our abilities? How can being new make us less creative, even if we know our relative newness is measured in minutes? In the rest of the chapter we'll explore a variety of reasons, most which revolve around both our inherited and learned fears of strangers, social rejection, and loss of social status.

THE ROLE OF BIOLOGY AND CULTURE:
WHY WE FEAR WHAT WE DON'T KNOW

Human beings are a product of two kinds of evolution: biological evolution that has shaped our brains and bodies, and cultural evolution that has taught us how to perceive, think about, and interact with others. For much of human history, being anxious and alert around strangers was beneficial. It helped us survive long enough to reproduce, and over time we've evolved to be nervous around unfamiliar people. For similar reasons, we've also evolved to fear rejection and the loss of social status in groups.

But there also was a survival advantage for early human groups who adopted "stranger danger" as a cultural norm. As a result, our *cultures* evolved to reinforce this natural fear of strangers. Even today, we're often *taught* at an early age to be anxious around unfamiliar people.

These early strategies were effective when meeting strangers and being new was rare. Prehistoric humans rarely met strangers, or found themselves starting and maintaining relationships with lots of people. Our ancestors were *very familiar* with the thirty to fifty members of their hunter-gatherer group, and perhaps a few dozen others in neighboring groups.[3] But outside of those individuals they probably interacted with few other people most days.[4] Since it took over a square mile of natural land to feed a single person, these hunter-gatherer groups were normally spaced many miles apart.[5]

Evolutionary biologist Robin Dunbar has compared the brain size of early humans with the brains and social networks of our primate cousins. Based on his research, he estimates that the average person in prehistoric times probably was aware of and had a loose connection with only about 150 people.[6] Extrapolated across a lifetime, that means that our ancestors probably encountered fewer than 300 to 400 strangers throughout *their entire lives.* Today, many of us encounter that many strangers every morning as we commute to work.

Early humans were rarely newcomers. Many of our ancestors grew up and lived their entire lives in a single hunter-gatherer clan, and *never* found themselves in a completely unfamiliar group. Others only became newcomers when they reached reproductive age, and either:

- Left on their own to find or join a mate (due to an instinctive desire *not* to mate with siblings and close relatives), or
- Were pushed out of their original group by rivals, or
- Were stolen, captured, or lured away by other groups looking for desirable mates.

As a result, there has been little evolutionary incentive for us to become really comfortable and confident meeting strangers and being new. Compared to other survival skills like hunting, fighting, and food-gathering, newcomer skills such as introducing ourselves and starting relationships were rarely used and surely didn't keep us alive on a daily basis. Historically, there has been a greater survival and reproductive advantage to fear strangers and avoid new situations than there has been to proactively seek out and join new groups.

YOUR CHALLENGE: OUT WITH OLD DEFENSES, IN WITH NEW STRATEGIES

All that has changed, and the problem for us is obvious. Our natural and learned stranger anxiety was mostly beneficial in a primitive world where encountering strangers was rare and often dangerous. But it's often counterproductive in a modern world where we're surrounded by strangers all the time and find we need to interact with unfamiliar people in order to gain the success and happiness we desire.

Hardwired by Genetic Evolution

To understand why we're anxious in new situations, we need to first understand a little bit about genetic and social evolution. Our DNA carries the genetic blueprint for creating our physical bodies. We inherited these genetic codes from our parents, who inherited them from their parents, and so on back through hundreds of generations. Indeed, it goes all the way back to the original single-celled organisms that were the first life on this planet.

From the beginning, random mutations sometimes gave certain individual organisms a survival advantage, increasing the chance they'd live long enough to mate and reproduce. Their offspring often inherited this advantageous DNA, and tended to survive and produce more offspring than those without it. Over time, the most beneficial genes (and the traits and abilities they help create) became more common in the organism's genetic code. Eventually, genetic evolution led to new species (including humans) who could think and act in ever more complex, sophisticated ways.

Learned Responses via Cultural Evolution

For much of early human history, our genetic code controlled our behavior, and we survived mostly by instinct.[7] Eventually we acquired the ability to learn from each other, and starting over 350,000 years ago, people not only passed on their genetic code to future generations but also their knowledge.[8]

If a group's technologies and cultural norms gave them a survival advantage relative to other groups, members of that group tended to produce, raise, and *teach* relatively more children. Over time, the most beneficial technical and cultural "mutations" also became more prevalent across human groups.

The Evolution of Newcomer and Stranger Anxiety

When you sense you're in a potentially dangerous situation, your brain secretes small amounts of hormones like adrenaline and cortisol, which help make you more alert and better prepared for "fight or flight." You also feel anxious. If you find yourself in real danger, your brain dumps even more hormones (and other chemicals) into your bloodstream, and temporarily this makes you stronger, quicker, and better able to flee or confront threats. You also feel fear.

Though this is a bit of an oversimplification, humans evolved to feel anxiety and fear because these emotions (and the physical changes associated with them) helped them either avoid or confront threats to their survival, and that eventually ensured their reproductive success.

Survival of the Fittest and Fear of Strangers

For much of human history, life has been a constant, competitive struggle for survival. There rarely was enough food, shelter, or mates to go around. Often only the strongest, most aggressive individuals lived long enough to reproduce equally strong, aggressive children who could continue passing on their genes to future generations. So, it's not surprising that we have evolved to be anxious around people who we think might:

- Injure and kill us (or our children).
- Take our food and shelter (and cause to starve to death or die of exposure).
- Take our most desirable mates (and thus reduce our chances of producing the best possible offspring).

Most hunter-gatherer groups rarely encountered unfamiliar people, especially ones outside of their tribe. When they did, there was a survival advantage to be anxious and aggressive toward strangers, because meeting them often meant that either they were encroaching upon your territory (and your resources) or you were encroaching upon theirs. In times of scarcity, it was often wise to assume the worst about strangers, and act accordingly.

As we invented tools, clothing, and language, our co-evolving cultures helped to reinforce positive, loyal feelings toward one's group, and cautious, antagonistic feelings toward other groups, especially unfamiliar ones. As one researcher put it, humans learned to "be nice to people who talk like you, dress like you, and act like you. Be suspicious of everyone else."[9] Over history, this cultural fear of strangers and newcomers sometimes has morphed into discrimination and xenophobia, permitting horrors like slavery and genocide.

Though none of us live in hunter-gatherer groups anymore, we've retained our ancestors' fear of strangers. According to child development experts, we're *born* with it. Researchers have found that babies start to tell the difference between familiar and unfamiliar people by the time they are two to four months old.[10] We start to be *anxious* around strangers by the time we're six months old.[11] Furthermore, scientists find little evidence to suggest that by six months we've learned this fear through either our initial experience or our parents.[12]

Whether we're born with a fear of strangers or not, most children show some level of nervousness around unfamiliar people, especially adults. Today, parents and teachers reinforce this anxiety by *teaching* us to fear and avoid unfamiliar people. Starting in the 1960s, school programs and public service ads on TV began warning children about "stranger danger" and the need to avoid interacting with unfamiliar adults who might lure them into dangerous situations.

While this is wise advice in general, researchers have found that children often internalize the message as either "*never* talk to strangers" or "*all* strangers are bad," and avoid seeking help when they need it. For example, in 2005, eleven-year-old Cub Scout Brennan Hawkins became lost on a camping trip. He was found alive four days later, but according to his parents his rescue was delayed because Brennan hid from would-be rescuers.

His mother told reporters that "He had two thoughts going through his head all the time," she said. "[His father] always told him that 'if you get lost, stay on the trail.' So he stayed on the trail. We've also told him 'don't talk to strangers.' . . . When an ATV or horse came by, he got off the trail. . . . When they left, he got back on the trail. . . . His biggest fear, he told me, was someone would steal him," she said.[13]

Though this was clearly an isolated incident, researchers have suggested that our fear of children being abducted by complete strangers doesn't quite match the evidence.[14] Still, our natural and cultural fear of strangers remains strong.

The Power of Groups and the Fear of Social Rejection

Long before humans arrived on the planet, animals also discovered that living and working together in groups could provide a survival and reproductive advantage. Individuals in groups can help each other:

- Hunt and find food.
- Build and maintain shelter.
- Watch out for and either avoid or confront predators.
- Protect and raise their young.
- Defend themselves and their resources from other groups.

In fact, groups provide such a survival and reproductive advantage that we've also evolved to fear being *rejected* by our group.[15] Though we don't exactly know how dangerous group rejection was long ago, we can infer it from what we see among our primate relatives. For example, when male rhesus monkeys leave or are pushed out of their birth group, over half of them die before they can get established in a new group. Some are killed by predators or die of starvation as they wander alone searching for other monkey groups. Others are injured or killed by established members as they try to integrate themselves into new groups.[16] Either way, the prospects for survival drop significantly when you're on your own in the wilderness.

These days, being rejected by a group rarely puts you in mortal danger, but you still retain that instinctive desire for belonging and natural fear of rejection. You may also have *learned* to be anxious as a result of your early childhood experiences, especially if you've ever found yourself:

- Excluded from play groups.
- Picked last for sports teams.
- Not invited to parties and social events.

Modern culture (especially TV and movies) can also promote and perpetuate the idea that social rejection mostly happens to dweebs, losers, and the uncool. Rejection might not be fatal these days, but we may fear it just as much as our cave dwelling ancestors did.

Status Hierarchies and the Fear of Losing Social Status

Though living together gave us a survival advantage, we still competed within our group for food, shelter, and mates. Often that competition turned violent, and we would end up injuring or killing each other as we fought for resources. Unfortunately, all that in-fighting hurt the group's collective chance for survival.

As a result, humans and other animals also have evolved the ability to create and maintain what researchers call *status hierarchies*. Rather than continually fight for power and dominance, group members develop a collective understanding of who is powerful, and who is not. Those with the most power or status get first choice of food, shelter, and mates, and those with low status wait their turn and settle for what remains. Members still compete with each other, but rivals only fight long enough to establish who is the strongest and most powerful.[17]

Over time, we've evolved to have a natural sensitivity to our relative social position in groups, and we fear losing status (and the access to the food, shelter, and mates that it implies). We're particularly anxious about status when:

- We are new to a group and our relative status is either unclear or still up for negotiation.
- Newcomers to our group threaten our existing status.
- We meet strangers and instinctively feel the need to establish our relative status differences.

Status hierarchies are clearly alive and well in modern society, and those with the most power and status still get the bigger and best share of everything. Many of us first experience competition for social status on the playground, and eventually in classrooms, sports teams, friendship groups, and the workplace. Early success and failure in these status contests also help shape how sensitive and worried we ultimately are about social status in new situations.

The challenge is that often our natural anxiety about losing social status is out of proportion with either the probability of it happening, or the true impact to our lives if it did. We've inherited a sensitivity and anxiety about social status from a prehistoric time where low status often meant starvation and death. These days losing social status is still something we don't desire, but it's rarely fatal.

In future chapters we'll see how our residual fear of strangers, group rejection, and loss of social status make us reluctant to introduce ourselves, ask questions, start relationships, and perform in front of unfamiliar people.

Civilization and the Rise of the Newcomer

Around 10,000 years ago, humans discovered that staying in one place to grow crops and raise animals was often a better survival strategy than foraging for food. Since agriculture could sustain more people per square mile, population density increased and people started to meet and interact with many more people than their ancestors did.[18]

New technologies and improved transportation allowed communities to trade food, tools, and other valuables with more distant tribes, increasing contact with strangers. The emerging benefits of division of labor also caused people to specialize in certain skills and trades, and sometimes move to new communities where their particular skill was in demand.

Over the next few thousand years (a blip by evolutionary standards), humans invented and established city states, trade routes, regional economies, standing armies, governments, schools, churches, and other institutions. Each of these changes dramatically increased the likelihood that people would meet strangers and find themselves newcomers to unfamiliar groups. Still, by the 1800s most people remained on farms or in small villages, occasionally encountering strangers, and were newcomers only a few times in their lives.

The industrial revolution changed everything. It brought thousands of people into densely packed cities, where they were surrounded by strangers all the time. People left farms and small artisan shops to become newcomer employees in factories, firms, and other organizations that had hundreds and sometimes thousands of workers.

City-dwellers began to interact with countless strangers while spending their money in stores, bars, restaurants, theaters, and other venues. People became frequent newcomers to schools, clubs, and volunteer organizations. Cars, trains, and subways allowed people to join thousands of strangers as they commuted to work, school, and leisure activities. Boats and planes permitted travel and migration to distant cities, and let everyone become newcomers to exotic cultures and lands. And now the Internet has created the possibility for us to meet practically everyone on the planet, and be newcomers to thousands of virtual groups.

Being new is less risky than ever, and, more important, the inherent risk of meeting strangers and joining new groups has dramatically changed. As we go about our day, most strangers we see or interact with these days are not encroaching on our territory or seeking to take our food, shelter, or mates. They are far more likely to be friendly and helpful than antagonistic and threatening.

Similarly, joining a new group these days is rarely a life-or-death situation, and often the worst that can happen to us is a bit of temporary embarrassment. Even if we are rejected by a group or find ourselves with low social status, there is almost always another group we can join. Despite this, we've inherited a prehistoric brain that is predisposed to be anxious around strangers and nervous in new situations.

One person I interviewed described his reaction to a new situation this way: "The rush of adrenaline was some sort of survival response to the fear that comes from knowing that I was in a place where I had little control. In fact, I felt like I was that species sitting at the bottom of the food chain."

We haven't evolved fast enough to be comfortable newcomers. Even though modern civilization and our global economy are built upon our ability to collaborate with strangers, we're still not that good at it. Our bodies and our cultures haven't evolved fast enough to meet the demands of modern society. As evolutionary psychologist Paul Seabright puts it:

> [M]odern society is an opportunistic experiment, founded on a human psychology that had already evolved before human beings had to deal with strangers in any systematic way.[19]

Fellow evolutionary psychologist Robert Wright also sees the mismatch between our evolutionary history and the demands of life today:

> We aren't designed to stand on crowded subway platforms, or to live in suburbs next door to people we never talk to, or to get hired or fired, or to watch the evening news. This disjunction between the contexts of our design and of our lives is probably responsible for much psychopathology, as well as much suffering of a less dramatic sort.[20]

Fortunately, there are ways for you to overcome your natural anxiety around strangers and new situations and become more comfortable, confident newcomers. Mindful reflection and deliberate practice can help you get better at introducing yourself, remembering names, asking questions, starting relationships, and performing in front of unfamiliar people.

FOUR

THE POWER OF PRACTICE AND REFLECTION

In this chapter we will explore why your past positive experiences aren't always enough to make you a comfortable newcomer. In particular, we'll look at:

- How you can recalibrate your inherited, learned anxieties to match the newcomer realities of the twenty-first century (instead of the Stone Age)
- Why practice and reflection are crucial to improvement and success
- Ways to overcome negative behavioral scripts and mindsets that hinder you from getting better and more comfortable at being new
- Various strategies that you can use to practice and improve your newcomer skills

By now it should not surprise you that most of us are anxious in new situations. We know how we got this way, but what can we do about it?

How can we overcome our genes and culture and become a more successful, confident, and less anxious newcomer?

PRESS THE RESET BUTTON: DON'T LET THE PAST CONTROL THE PRESENT

Unfortunately, you won't become a better, more confident newcomer just by reading this book. No one has permanently lost weight by reading a diet book, or gotten in shape by buying an exercise book. Reading this book is a good first step, but to really become a more comfortable, confident newcomer you need to do two things:

1. You need to find opportunities to *practice* and get better at the five newcomer skills.
2. You need to mindfully *reflect* on your newcomer experiences and recalibrate your brain so that you don't automatically overestimate the social risk you're taking in new situations.

You'll never remove all your newcomer anxieties. In fact, you shouldn't; some caution in new situations is a good thing. But you can learn to reduce your anxieties through practice and reflection, accept what nervousness remains, and push beyond it to seek out and embrace the new experiences that ultimately bring the success and happiness you want.

Avoid Complacency: Each Challenge Is an Opportunity to Improve

In order to see why practice and reflection are important, you first need to understand why all the experience and "practice" you've had until now hasn't already made you a confident, comfortable newcomer. Throughout your life, it is likely you have been in hundreds of newcomer situations and have interacted with thousands of strangers. Most

of those interactions have gone well; your worst fears rarely materialized. Why, then, with all that experience, haven't you already gained
the practice you need to be good at the five newcomer skills and have
recalibrated your Stone Age brain so that you're not more anxious than
you should be in new situations?

Psychologist K. Anders Ericsson and his colleagues have spent decades exploring the science of performance. They have sought to understand why some people eventually become really good at certain things,
while others seem to quickly plateau and never get beyond average performance. Over the years they've studied everyone from fighter pilots to
athletes, musicians, chess masters, and high-speed touch typists,[1] and
found that once most people reach some reasonable, functional level of
performance at a particular task, they often start paying less and less attention to how they perform. Eventually they come to perform the task
without thinking—that is, without mindful reflection—yet without it
they don't continue to improve over time.

Driving is a good example. While we're learning to drive we're very
aware of our performance, but once we've accumulated a few hundred
hours behind the wheel, we spend less and less time paying conscious
attention to our driving. Instead, we listen to the radio, think about our
day, or worse yet, pull out the smartphone to call, text, or read emails.
Eventually one day we suddenly discover we've traveled miles down
the road and can't remember anything about our journey. Sound familiar?

Avoid the Behavioral Script Trap; Take Yourself off Autopilot

Some of this occurs naturally when we create what researchers call behavioral scripts.[2] In order to simplify our lives, our minds create little
behavioral programs that we automatically launch in certain situations
so we don't have to think much about what we're doing. When we wake
up in the morning, we trigger scripts to brush our teeth in a particular

way, or read the newspaper in a certain order. As we move through the day, we launch scripts to commute to work, check email, get lunch, and so on.

We also create scripts for our social interactions with others, including newcomer situations. Think about what you normally do when you walk into a party or social event filled mostly with strangers. Some of us automatically seek out the host or another friendly face, and initially focus on socializing with people we know. Some of us head straight for the refreshment table to ensure we're not the only person without a drink in our hand. As we begin to interact with new people, some of us proactively approach others, while some wait for others to approach them. Usually we trigger these behavioral scripts without thinking, and over time they become unquestioned habits.

The trick, then, becomes changing the script and breaking the habit. From interviews with many people who overcame their newcomer anxieties and learned to be more comfortable and confident in new situations, I've learned that, in almost every case, it took a pivotal experience that forced them to practice the newcomer skills and recalibrate their expectations of what the likely outcome of a new situation might be.

The Pivotal Moment: Do the Thing that Scares You
One newcomer I interviewed characterized himself as growing up fairly shy and introverted. Here's how he described a party he attended:

> "When I was in eighth grade I went to a social event attended by ninth graders. I didn't know anyone. I walked in, went straight to the back of the room, and stared at a bookcase for three hours. There were thirty kids there. My buddy, who was a year older, invited me, and I thought I could handle it, but he went off on his own without making any introductions. It was a new situation that really went awry. I was uncomfortable in new situations from an early age. I

didn't interact. It's always been hard for me when there are three or more people. I get overwhelmed."

His pivotal moment came soon after graduating from college when he took a sales job at a financial services company:

> "When I told my parents that I would be on the phone five hours a day selling, they said, 'We can't understand you over the phone; you mumble. How can you sell?' The job fell into my lap. I didn't know what I wanted, but it was a good company, so I took it. It was a long process but I overcame the challenge; it forced me to develop my interpersonal skills. . . . I'm still an introvert. It's come with a lot of practice."

I asked him how his sales job made him a more comfortable newcomer:

> "I was forced to talk to a lot of people and build rapport with them. It was very exhausting, but it forced me to interact. If I had a bad call, if someone hung up on me, I just dialed again. I didn't get bruised once I realized it was a numbers game. I learned not to take it personally, and overcame my fear of rejection. You learn that you don't really change that much when you're rejected anyway."

The sales job not only gave him the practice to improve his newcomer skills, it also helped him recalibrate his brain so he didn't see meeting and interacting with strangers as such a risky thing.

Another person I interviewed also transformed himself into someone others see as quite comfortable in new situations:

> "I'm actually very shy and introverted. I see myself as more introverted than my friends do. On a [extroversion] scale of 1 to 10, I rate myself a 2 or 3, but my friends perceive me as a 6."

His pivotal moment came when he went on his Mormon mission to Brazil. When members of the Mormon faith graduate from high school, most are trained and sent somewhere in the world for a year to spread the faith, which involves visiting neighborhoods and knocking on doors. As you might imagine, this experience provides lots of practice in introducing oneself, asking questions, starting relationships, and performing in front of unfamiliar people. All that practice not only helped him improve his newcomer skills, it also helped him recalibrate how he viewed strangers and the risk of social rejection:

> "My wife says I'm a great 'home base' [at parties], as I'm not afraid to meet new people. After meeting two to three thousand people and being rejected a lot, it became easier. I hoped that I wouldn't be, but I'd tell myself that if I met a hundred people, my goal would be to connect with four or five really good people that I could help out. I flipped the notion, and reset my expectations."

He is still surprised that he's willing to move to new locations and put himself into new situations:

> "I lost my fear of many things. . . . I was in Philadelphia for two years, Brazil for four months; four years in Boston is the longest I've ever lived [in one place], which is weird. I'm OK moving to find the best opportunities. . . . Before the mission I was very shy and timid, and I bet without the mission I would still be living within ten to fifteen miles of where I grew up."

Avoid the Mental Model Trap: Question Your Beliefs

Along with behavioral scripts, we also come to develop mental models about being new that help us anticipate what might happen when we encounter and start interacting with unfamiliar people and groups.[3]

Some aspects of our mental models come from the instincts we're born with, inherited from our parents and distant ancestors. Others come from our early childhood experiences and what we learn from parents and teachers.

Regardless of how they develop, our mental models about being new tend to stabilize and solidify over time. We come to acquire and often subconsciously hold a set of unquestioned assumptions and expectations about how strangers and new groups will:

- React to our initial approach.
- Respond to our questions and requests.
- Create first impressions about us.
- Welcome and accept us.

Pivotal Moment: Test Your Assumptions

A woman I interviewed was introverted and shy in high school: "I wouldn't go to a party unless my close friends were going, too. Once there, I talked only to them. I never talked to someone new, it wouldn't happen." What transformed her was spending her junior year abroad:

> "It changed my life! I went to Spain because I spoke Spanish, thought I was good at it, and had declared it as my major. I wanted to be fluent, so I bit the bullet and pushed myself. I thought a year was too long, but I forced myself to go. During the weeks leading up to it, I kept telling myself I wasn't getting on the plane. But I somehow I did."

Initially she was extremely reluctant to speak Spanish and interact with strangers. After a few weeks, her host sat her down and bluntly told her: "This isn't going to work. You have to start talking. You are never going to learn if you don't talk to anyone. No one is going to care or make fun of you if you are weak in Spanish. You have to try."

In the following months she overcame her fear of speaking Spanish with strangers and started traveling throughout Spain and the rest of Europe on weekends and holidays. Living and traveling in a foreign country put her into countless newcomer situations, giving her lots of opportunities to practice the five newcomer skills. It also helped her re-calibrate her brain and enter other types of new situations with less anx-iety about asking questions and making mistakes. She ultimately realized:

> "It's only as scary as you let it be. You have to get used to being new. I was there ten months and I should have gotten used to it ear-lier. . . . You have to get past who you are inside and take more chances. You'll only get used to something if you suck it up and try it. It's hard to get used to something unless you put yourself out there."

Note: Don't assume from these examples that in order to become a more comfortable, confident newcomer you have to take a job you don't want or board a plane to someplace strange and exotic. But you do need to put yourself into situations that give you opportunities to practice your newcomer skills. You also have to take the time to reflect on your expe-riences and adjust your expectations and assumptions so that you don't automatically become nervous and reluctant to approach strangers.

No Reflection, No Improvement

The good thing about behavioral scripts and mental models is that they make life possible. Without them we'd have to constantly think about every little thing we do. We'd be overwhelmed with information, and multitasking would be impossible. Being a newcomer would be espe-cially challenging; we always would have to struggle to make sense of and respond to highly uncertain social situations.

The downside of scripts and mental models is that they often lock us into a way of thinking and acting that:

- Is less effective than it could be.
- Causes us more anxiety than we should have under the circumstances.
- Makes us reluctant to pursue the opportunities that will bring us the success and happiness we want.

More specifically, our unquestioned scripts and mental models can keep us from taking the initiative to:

- Introduce ourselves.
- Ensure we learn and remember names.
- Ask questions.
- Start relationships.
- Perform in front of unfamiliar people.

What's worse, our mental models can condition us to feel and act a certain way in new situations. If we automatically fear the worst and assume we won't enjoy being new, and think and act based on these expectations, we're likely to get the experience we expect. This effectively creates a self-fulfilling prophecy that only reinforces those expectations the next time.[4]

Without observing and reflecting upon our behavioral scripts, or examining and challenging our mental models, we have little hope of breaking out of our mindless habits and assumptions and seeing real improvement.

THE POWER OF DELIBERATE PRACTICE

When it comes to improving performance, K. Anders Ericsson and his colleagues have found that neither raw talent nor the total number of hours of experience ultimately predicts which people become expert, world-class performers and which ones don't. Instead, they've found that people who continue to improve their performance engage in what they call deliberate practice,[5] meaning they make a commitment to be much more observant, reflective, and mindful of their performance. More specifically, world-class performers tend to:

- First imagine what improved performance looks like and what they want to achieve.
- Break down their overall performance into its underlying set of specific behaviors and skills.
- Systematically focus on improvement by mindfully observing themselves perform that specific behavior (and asking others for feedback on it, too).
- Identify ways to improve and then find or create opportunities to experiment with new approaches.
- Continue to practice, observe, and get feedback from others until they see real improvement.
- Shift focus to other associated behaviors and skills and keep repeating the process until they achieve the overall performance they desire.

Contrary to what you might have heard about practice in general, it doesn't take 10,000 hours to get better at being new.[6] This number (also based on research by K. Anders Ericsson and his associates) refers to the average amount of practice required to become world-class performers, or the top 0.1 of 1 percent. Most of us don't have the desire (or probably even the talent) to become a world-champion newcomer. If you're like me, just being above average would be great. To achieve this more modest goal it may only take a few hours of mindful, deliberate practice on the five newcomer skills for you to see a real difference on how you think and act when you're new.

THE POWER OF MINDFUL REFLECTION
AND RECALIBRATION

In addition to practicing, the key to becoming a more confident and less anxious newcomer is to recalibrate your prevailing assumptions and expectations about being new so that you don't automatically become more nervous and reluctant in new situations than is necessary or beneficial.

For years, psychologists have been helping people overcome excessive and counterproductive anxieties and fears through a technique called *cognitive-behavioral therapy*.[7] This approach doesn't involve endless hours on the couch exploring childhood trauma or your relationship with your mother. It doesn't even necessarily require a therapist.

To use this technique to become a more confident, less anxious newcomer you simply need to:

- Notice and reflect upon the worries, anxieties, and reluctance you feel when you're new.
- Find opportunities to put yourself into new situations and practice the tasks you're most nervous about (e.g., introducing yourself, asking questions, performing in front of unfamiliar people, etc.).
- Compare what you imagined would happen to what actually transpired.
- Over time, adjust your in-going assumptions and expectations so that you don't automatically fear things that rarely happen or have much less negative impact than you think.

The goal of this approach is not to eliminate all anxiety, but to adjust your mental models so that you're not more nervous than you really need (or should) be in new situations.

APPROACH BEING NEW WITH A NEW MINDSET

Over the next five chapters, we will systematically examine each new-comer skill, striving to:

- Understand why we get anxious and reluctant to perform it when we're new.
- Explore strategies and approaches to become more confident and effective at doing it.
- Identify opportunities and exercises to mindfully, deliberately practice and get better at it.
- Reflect upon and compare our assumptions and expectations about performing it with what actually happens (to help recalibrate our mental models).

To get better at being new, sometimes it can help to approach these efforts with one or more of the following mindsets:

The Scientist Mindset

When it comes to practice and improvement, we're often our own worst enemies. We fixate on every mistake and stumble, and assume the worst in terms of how others see our performance. If it helps, you can approach your improvement effort as if you were a scientist studying yourself. That way, you can:

- Enter new situations with more curiosity than fear.
- Take a more detached, objective view of both your performance and the emotions you feel (before, during, and after).
- View your improvement efforts as experiments rather than all-or-nothing tests of your ability.

The Coach Mindset

Since each of the five newcomer skills is a social performance, sometimes it can help to step outside yourself and pretend you're a professional coach helping you train for your next newcomer "track meet." With a coach's mindset, you can:

- Enter new situations with the goal of getting better through practice and feedback.
- Like the scientist, take a more detached, professional view of your newcomer performance.
- View and design improvement efforts as workouts and drills that over time will help build your newcomer capabilities.

The Gamer Mindset

Often we take ourselves way too seriously, and we imagine every new situation as a high-stakes, make-or-break test of our talent. Sometimes it can help to approach new situations as if they were social video games. That way, you can:

- Approach new situations as a fun, exciting challenge.
- Focus more on navigating and succeeding in the "social gaming environment" than fixating on your fears and anxieties.
- Recognize that mistakes might cause you to "lose a few social points," but you can almost always hit the replay button and try again.

The Beginner Mindset

Another beneficial strategy can be to approach the newcomer skills as if you have never done them before. Zen Buddhists call this adopting a Beginner's Mind,[8] and with this perspective you can:

- Enter new situations with the excitement and anticipation of learning something new.
- Be more open-minded and sensitive to new perspectives and ideas.
- Accept your inevitable stumbles as "beginner's mistakes" instead of permanent disabilities.

You don't have to adopt any of these mindsets to see improvement. But if you think they might help you stay focused on getting better, give them a try.

BECOMING A COMPETENT NEWCOMER

The goal of all this practice and reflection is to help you uncover and explore all your assumptions, expectations, habits, and abilities associated with being new, and then find ways to adjust and improve them so you eventually become a more comfortable, confident newcomer in any situation.

Learning expert Noel Burch describes this journey as passing through four stages.[9] We start in a state of *unconscious incompetence*, mindlessly muddling through newcomer situations without much thought to our emotions and abilities. By starting to observe and reflect, you can begin to transition toward *conscious incompetence*, becoming aware (and accepting that) there is room for improvement.

By practicing some of the techniques and exercises, you can eventually shift toward *conscious competence*, and see real improvement in your newcomer abilities, especially when you pay attention to and make a real effort to perform them well. Ultimately, your improved newcomer skills and mindsets will make their way into your behavioral scripts and mental models, and you'll move closer to a state of *unconscious competence*.

As you set off on your journey:

1. *Decide what type of newcomer you want to be.* Create a personal vision for yourself and decide how you *want* to think, act, and feel in new situations.

2. *Make a public commitment.* Researchers have shown that if you tell your co-workers, friends, and family that you're trying to improve, you're more likely to stick with it and see real progress.[10]

3. *Observe and model the behaviors of confident, effective newcomers.* Identify people you think are pretty good at being new, and watch how they introduce themselves, ask questions, start relationships, and so on. See what you can copy and imitate to get better yourself.

4. *Be patient.* Remember that you're trying to uncover and change habits, assumptions, and expectations that have been with you for most of your life. While you might quickly read and understand what's in this book, it'll take much longer to practice, refine, and internalize new behaviors and mental models. Sometimes as you pay attention to and practice one specific newcomer skill, you find you'll momentarily get worse at another skill. Have the confidence that over time it'll all come together and your overall performance will improve.

5. *Relax and have fun with this.* It's unlikely that your next newcomer situation will be *the* pivotal moment that defines your ultimate life and career success. So don't treat it as such. You're better off approaching new situations with curiosity and a *c'est la vie* attitude than with fear and trepidation.

———

Good luck!

Part 2

MASTERING THE FIVE CRITICAL NEWCOMER SKILLS

In this section we'll systematically explore each newcomer skill, first understanding why the skill is important to success and why it causes so much stress and anxiety. Then we'll review strategies to become more sucessful and confident in the skill, and explore ways to reflect upon, practice, and get better at it.

FIVE

INTRODUCING YOURSELF

In this chapter we will explore our reluctance to introduce ourselves to new people, and discover how to improve our ability to:

- Approach strangers with less anxiety.
- Introduce ourselves with confidence.
- Make a good first impression.
- Engage in small talk that helps establish a positive relationship.
- Leave introductions feeling more comfortable and willing to approach others later.

All successful relationships start with introductions, and we all know that introductions—whether we introduce ourselves or others introduce us— are important. But many of us are reluctant to introduce ourselves despite all the benefits that flow from introductions. Instead, many of the people I've interviewed say they wait to be introduced, or wait for others to approach them.

BENEFITS OF GETTING TO KNOW ONE ANOTHER

In the job market, being introduced or introducing yourself often leads to learning about job opportunities and making the connections you need to get an initial interview. Once you're hired and start working, introductions act as a "permission slip" to gain access to the information, help, and advice you need to be successful in your new role. As one newcomer put it, "It's who you know that counts, and you have so much more mileage if you have already been introduced." To that I would add "or if you have introduced yourself." Introductions also help you build social connections to co-workers that make you feel accepted and satisfied at work.

Outside the office, introductions or introducing yourself help you:

- Start friendly relationships with neighbors, classmates, and other parents, among many others. These relationships allow you and those you meet to socialize, share information, commiserate about life's challenges, and find ways to help each other. Some word introductions may lead to deep, enduring friendships you will cherish throughout your life.
- Build more friendly and productive relationships with bank tellers, waiters, cashiers, sales clerks, and other people with whom you regularly interact, which make those frequent exchanges more personal and pleasant, and often lead to better service.
- Make temporary encounters, such as airplane rides, bus tours, volunteer projects, concerts, sporting events, and even commuting more relaxed, comfortable, and enjoyable. All it takes is one person willing to introduce him- or herself, and suddenly there is lively conversation, banter, and joking among total strangers that brings energy to everyone involved and makes time fly.

Behavioral scientists Nicholas Epley and Juliana Schroeder demonstrated this with a simple experiment. They asked one group of commuters to introduce themselves to whomever sat next to them on the train one morning. They asked another group to follow their normal routine. They found that "commuters who talked to a stranger reported a more positive experience than those who sat in solitude."[1] The benefit was the same for both extroverts and introverts.[2] This was the opposite of what other commuters at the train station predicted.

Overall, much of the success and happiness we desire at work and in life starts with introductions.

LACK OF INTRODUCTIONS AND THE S.N.O.W. JOB

Most newcomers recognize that it's often unwise to wait for others to take the initiative. But despite their best intentions to approach strangers and introduce themselves to others, they lose courage in the heat of the moment. The experiences of two people I interviewed are typical; the first described a cocktail party:

> "I'm not good at this for the most part. I'm likely to wait for someone to speak to me. I might linger at the bar or play with my phone until someone approaches me, which isn't always the best strategy. It says a lot about me; I need to be more proactive, but introductions take work. If it's someone I know is key to my work, I may go ahead and introduce myself, but, even then, I often prefer to wait."

On his second day on the job, the other newcomer got tired of reading initial project materials. He attempted to introduce himself to his new co-workers, but couldn't overcome his reluctance to approach and interrupt busy people:

> "That was around 8:25 or so. I sat there reading, first because I wanted to, then later because I had been there for so long and I couldn't think of anything better to do till 10:45. I decided: "Enough is enough. I'm going to meet some people." I walked around. My

two supervisor figures were on the phone. My future co-workers were in their cubes either reading or doing computer stuff. I lost nerve and went back and read."

Of course, we all hope our managers, teachers, guides, or hosts will take us around and properly introduce us to everyone in the group. If they don't, we hope that others will automatically recognize and meet their obligation to approach and welcome us onboard. But over half of the people I've interviewed have been dissatisfied with either the number or quality of introductions they've received, especially at work.

Many tell a similar story: on their first day the boss quickly ushers them around the office, making a rapid-fire series of hello-and-handshake introductions with those who happen to be around. Once it's over, the newcomers usually have forgotten the names of everyone they met, and they don't really feel connected to anyone.

Even worse, some newcomers get the "Hey, Everybody" treatment. The boss stands up in front of the entire department and says, "Hey, everybody, this is Bill. Everyone say hi!" Managers who use this approach think they've done their duty, but that kind of introduction is probably worse than no introduction at all.

Whether owing to manager or host incompetence, bad manners on the part of our new group mates, or our own newcomer reluctance, the lack of early, high-quality introductions causes two major problems. First, we don't feel we've made strong enough connections to feel comfortable approaching others for help and advice later. As a result, we don't get up to speed quickly, are less productive, and feel like an outsider for much longer than we need to be.

Second, if we don't introduce ourselves or receive an introduction the first time we see or interact with someone, it's often much more awkward and embarrassing the next time. If we continue to run into each other without introducing ourselves, we can find ourselves giving each other what I've come to call the Smile, Nod, Or Wave treatment, or "S.N.O.W. Job." We politely acknowledge each other's presence with a smile, nod, or wave, or even exchange a few words of greeting or small talk. But we're both too embarrassed to move past bland pleasantries and really get to know each other.

FRIEND OR FOE? WHAT YOU CAN LEARN ABOUT INTRODUCTIONS FROM THE TUAREG

The Tuareg are nomadic livestock herders in northern Africa. If you're traveling alone in the desert, strangers can be welcome human contact and an important source of information about nearby food and water. Strangers can also rob and kill you. As a result, the Tuareg have developed very sophisticated rituals designed to help them determine whether the camel-riding stranger they see in the distance is friend or foe. If the other person doesn't follow these rituals, it's a sign the person is not part of their extended group and potentially hostile, or at least someone not to be trusted.

The Tuareg have specific rules for how to approach strangers from afar, and have norms for sizing up distant riders based on camel type, saddle, and riding style. Once they ultimately meet, the visitor or newcomer must begin the introduction. There are even rules by which to determine who the newcomer is in specific situations.

For example, following a traditional greeting, they exchange a handshake. Then there is a complex set of questions and responses that both parties need to follow before they can begin a general conversation, as well as specific rules for how to end the encounter and go their separate ways.

These rituals help both parties manage "stranger risk" by evaluating and demonstrating friendly intent from the first visual contact all the way to a face-to-face meeting. This allows them to take advantage of potentially productive desert encounters, while giving them more time (and distance) to avoid potentially dangerous ones.[3]

Your interactions with strangers rarely—if ever—have the high-stakes, life-or-death risk of a desert encounter. But introductions are still a way of initially determining whether a new person is someone you want to continue interacting with or someone you'd prefer to avoid. Our initial uncertainty around strangers, coupled with our natural and learned fear of unfamiliar people, is one reason we're often anxious and uncomfortable introducing ourselves in new situations.

THE UNCLEAR ETIQUETTE OF SELF-INTRODUCTIONS: NORMS AND SOCIAL ACCEPTANCE

In modern society, our reluctance to introduce ourselves also comes from our fear of violating norms and expectations around self-introductions. Through my interviews I've found that most of us worry more about the social risk of introducing ourselves than with the physical risk of meeting strangers. We worry about:

- Approaching and interrupting people at the wrong time and place
- Introducing ourselves to people who don't want to meet us
- Not having a good enough reason for introducing ourselves
- Saying something to annoy, anger, offend, or generally make a bad first impression

Why do we care so much about following social norms concerning things like introductions? Once again, this goes back to our inherited and learned fear of social rejection. Long ago our ancestors realized that if they banded together in groups and helped each other, they had a better chance of surviving and reproducing. But how do you ensure that everyone does his or her part for group success?

One way is to develop social norms around beneficial and helpful behaviors and then make performing them a requirement for joining and staying in the group. People who demonstrate these norms are accepted as insiders, and those who don't are scorned and either pushed or kept out of the group.

Given that in prehistoric times group rejection was a dangerous outcome, it's not surprising that we've evolved to instinctively fear the violation of social norms, including those associated with introductions. In theory, we could minimize this social risk by simply learning and mastering the prevailing social norms for introducing ourselves. Etiquette should provide the answers, but unfortunately in today's world it doesn't quite work out that way. We don't actually *have* clear, prevailing social norms for self-introductions, and the resulting uncertainty only makes us more reluctant to introduce ourselves.

When, Where, and How to Introduce Yourself

Crazy as it seems, there are no official etiquette rules for how and when to introduce ourselves to others. I've examined most of the popular etiquette books published today, and none have clear, specific guidelines for self-introductions.

There are plenty of etiquette guidelines for introducing *other* people, though. For example, the latest edition of *Emily Post's Etiquette* devotes over twenty-two pages to making and receiving introductions.[4] There are separate sections explaining in detail how to properly introduce co-workers, parents, children, domestic partners, military officers, and even royalty and heads of state. The book also covers how to introduce one person to a group, what to say if you've been incorrectly introduced, and even how to properly shake hands with the disabled. But there are only a few sentences on self-introductions, and they offer relatively little help. For example:

> It may take a little courage to approach someone you don't know, but introducing yourself is really one of the easiest introductions. After all, you only have to remember your own name. At large social events, it's impossible for hosts to introduce everyone, so be prepared to introduce yourself. Even in the most formal setting, self-introductions

are expected and relatively casual. "Hello, I'm Justin Vail" is usually enough to start a simple reply.[5]

If introducing yourself is really one of the easiest introductions, why do we get so anxious about it? It might be appropriate and expected at a party or networking event, but is there always a good reason to introduce yourself? Will the other person recognize and see it as appropriate, too? If you're joining a work group, you obviously have a good reason to introduce yourself to your new teammates. But what about people who just happen to work in the same building? Or who sit next to you on a long airplane ride? Or come to the same aerobics class? Is just being friendly enough of a reason to introduce yourself? There are no clear answers, and I believe the social uncertainty it creates increases our reluctance to approach others.

Even if we have a good reason, it's also unclear when and where it's appropriate to introduce ourselves. For example, at work it's clearly rude to introduce yourself to people while they are talking on the phone or going to the bathroom. But what if they are working diligently at their desks? Eating lunch in the cafeteria? Standing next to you in the elevator? Walking down the hallway? Each of those situations has a different feel for appropriateness, but there are no clear guidelines (in society or etiquette books). Once again, that uncertainty adds to our anxiety.

Given all this social fuzziness, it's not surprising that we often wait for others to approach and introduce themselves to us. By doing so we let other people take the social risk, and let them worry about having a good reason and the right timing. The problem is that other people likely think and act the same way you do. As a result, you both end up waiting for the other person to make the first move, and in the meantime, you're filling your limited interactions with smiles, nods, waves, and polite small talk.

———

Fortunately, now that you understand the genetic and cultural reasons underlying why we're reluctant to introduce ourselves to strangers, let's look at a few strategies and techniques for how to approach and engage unfamiliar people, so that you can become better and more comfortable when introducing yourself.

GO AHEAD AND DO IT: THE SOCIAL RISK
IS (ALMOST) ALWAYS LESS THAN YOU THINK

For something as simple as introducing ourselves, we're up against thousands of years of evolution and a life of learning to be fearful of strangers and social rejection. We want all the good things that come from self-introductions, and our managers, parents, and teachers expect us to put ourselves out there and introduce ourselves to new people. Still, we worry about how other people will react, and unless it's absolutely necessary, we often choose to wait for an introduction that frequently never comes.

But when I interview newcomers about their thoughts and emotions around self-introductions, I often find an interesting contradiction. Many newcomers describe their reluctance to approach and introduce themselves to busy, important people, and they worry about having a good reason. But when I ask how they react *when someone else approaches them*, they're usually quite happy to stop what they're doing and get acquainted. Here's how one newcomer put it:

> "It's harder when I have to introduce myself and then ask for something. But when people introduce themselves to me and then ask for a favor I have no problem, but why the reverse is an issue I don't know."

I've never heard anyone tell me they usually get offended or annoyed when people come up and introduce themselves. No one I've interviewed has ever said:

> "Can you imagine the nerve of that new hire? Last week he came up and introduced himself as if he owned the place. Of course, I yelled

at him, chased him away, and went and told the boss to fire the jerk immediately."

Yet somehow in the back of our minds we imagine this is a likely outcome of introducing ourselves. So your initial move toward becoming more comfortable and confident in making introductions is to accept the following idea: The social risk of approaching and introducing yourself to a stranger is usually much less than you think. It's something we'll revisit in some form throughout this book.

To prove my point, let me ask you a question. Think back to the last few times when newcomers approached you and introduced themselves. How did you feel? What did you do? Was your first instinct to get angry or to laugh as they stumbled through their introductions? Were you really annoyed or bothered by the interruption? Or, did you stop what you were doing, enthusiastically welcome them to the organization, and get to know them a little bit?

Assuming you are relatively normal (which you probably are), why would you expect anyone else to feel differently if you approached them? Of course, we can always point to the grouches who bite the heads off anyone who interrupts their precious routines, but they're rare and probably no one values their opinion anyway.

Here's the advice of a self-proclaimed introvert I interviewed who, through reflection and practice, transformed himself into someone who is now comfortable and confident with self-introductions:

"Yes, I had anxiety when I was a teenager, but not now. As an adult I don't have a problem approaching strangers. I actually enjoy doing it. It's easy to learn a lot by talking with people. I had fear in my late teens and early 20s but came to realize that the worst-case scenario was that someone might ignore me, or not be interested in talking, or might just be a complete jerk.

If the worst did happen, there were always others to talk to. I came to weigh the worst-case scenario against the best-case scenario and there was no comparison. I could gain so much and potentially lose so little. The worst case was nothing. If you don't try you'll never know. It's really the only way to go."

Based on all my research, my advice is:

- Accept that your reluctance to introduce yourself is completely normal.
- Don't fixate on the worst that can happen in an introduction; it rarely does.
- Just go ahead and introduce yourself.

BEGIN AT THE BEGINNING: IDENTIFY WHOM YOU WANT TO MEET

It sounds simple, but the first step toward overcoming your reluctance and pushing forward is to figure out whom you want to introduce yourself to. Just having a strategy and plan can reduce your anxiety and give you more confidence as you face a sea of strangers. Sometimes it feels like you have just a few moments to formulate a plan, such as when you walk into a networking event or party. But in most newcomer situations you have plenty of time to plot and strategize who, where, when, and in what order you want to introduce yourself. There is rarely one perfect strategy—you just need one that gives you the confidence to take action and approach somebody.

At work, there is usually a key group of co-workers who can provide the help, resources, and advice you need to get your work done. Some may be easily identified, but think broadly:

- Team members on your initial project, including those from other functions
- Other co-workers in your group or department

- Key support people like administrative assistants, HR managers, technicians, and facilities staff
- The boss of your boss, and any other managers who monitor or make decisions that directly affect your work

There also are those less obvious but still important people:

- People who used to work on your initial project, technology, sales region, and so on—they know what's been tried before and who else might have critical information
- The go-to people in the department (every group has at least one) who know the most about the products, technologies, and services, or who are the most connected to those who do know
- Key customers and clients (external or internal) who can provide you the user's perspective on your projects

Finally, there are those people not directly connected to your daily work, but whom you'll run into or interact with frequently:

- Office neighbors (especially on the same floor)
- Receptionists
- Security guards
- Janitors
- Cafeteria workers

Take the time to introduce yourself to these people when you're new. Avoid the "smile and nod" relationship (which could have been avoided if you'd just introduced yourself right away) with a receptionist, janitor, or security guard. They probably know more about what really goes on in the company and how to get things done than many of the managers do.

Of course, don't just limit yourself to your initial list; there will be plenty of people you'll randomly run into who aren't clearly connected to your project or office location. You don't want to be the office politician and shake-and-howdy everyone you see, but if it seems appropriate, introduce yourself.

Outside of work, the same strategies apply. Go beyond the obvious and those seated or standing next to you, and seek out those who can really help you succeed, as well as all the people you know you'll interact with frequently as a newcomer.

Remember this: *The nice thing about being new is you have the implicit right, permission, and justification to introduce yourself to just about anyone.*

————

If you're walking into a group of unfamiliar people, and you have some choice about who you can approach, here's some good advice from one newcomer I interviewed:

> "I try not to interrupt. I'll look for those standing alone. I'll look for other people who seem lost. Some of my best friends were met when they were also holding back trying to take it all in. They were just grateful someone came up and spoke to them."

REMEMBER YOUR GOAL: TO START A RELATIONSHIP

The key to successful self-introductions is to recognize that the goal of any introduction is to start a relationship. The relationship might end up lasting a few minutes or a lifetime, but either way it's a relationship. How and when you approach someone, and what you say during the introduction, are largely based on what you think that future relationship might be.

There are many types of relationships, including:

- Group members (same department, project, committee, class, church, etc.)
- Authority figures (boss, teacher, minister, police officer, etc.)

- Co-participants (same flight, party, concert, ski lift, elevator, etc.)
- Co-habitants (neighbor, nearby cubicle dweller, etc.)
- Customers and clients (your provide them products or services, or vice versa)

Some relationships will be important for work and life success; some will be necessary evils; and some will just be nice to have. While a few relationships will blossom into really strong collaborations or deep friendships, many will not (for a variety of reasons).

You are justifiably nervous meeting your new boss, team members, neighbors, dorm mates, or new in-laws. You want to make a good first impression because you'll be interacting with them a lot over the next few months and years. But recognize that over time you'll also have a second, hundredth, and likely a ten thousandth impression, and the long-term social risk of that initial introduction is probably pretty small.

It's best to think of other types of relationships as a numbers game. In most social situations involving co-participants, co-habitants, and customer/clients, there are many people you can introduce yourself to. If one approach and self-introduction doesn't go well, smile, shrug your shoulders, and move on to the next one. Recognize that you're hard-wired and socialized to see more long-term social risk in these random introductions than there really is.

SELF-INTRODUCTIONS: THE APPROACH AND OPENING LINES

You will feel more confident and comfortable introducing yourself if you spend some time thinking about and experimenting with approach strategies and opening lines. The more you reflect and practice, the easier and less stressful self-introductions will become.

Don't be overly concerned about when and where to approach someone to introduce yourself; there are usually multiple opportunities. In face-to-face introductions, you can often introduce yourself before or after group activities and meetings, during random hallway and parking lot encounters, or while the person is alone and at his or her desk.

Waiting for the perfect time to introduce yourself is almost always counterproductive. Don't interrupt someone who is performing brain surgery or going to the bathroom, but otherwise approach the person the first moment you feel you can successfully get his or her attention. Ask yourself if you'd be willing to be interrupted if you were doing what that person is doing. If so, go for it. You can use your opening lines to confirm whether this is a good time. If it isn't, find a better time later.

There are many ways to begin a self-introduction, but most effective opening lines generally follow this route:

1. Lead with a greeting: "Hi, good morning," and so on.
2. Follow with your name.
3. Establish the interaction as an introduction.
4. Very briefly state who you are and why you're introducing your-self (based upon what kind of relationship you're expecting to develop). Ideally you would also tell the person that you're new. Ask permission to continue the introduction, or find a better time to complete it.
5. Be brief and quickly give the other person a chance to respond.

You can tailor the opening lines based on who you're meeting and any prior information you have about the other person. For example, suppose new hire Marilyn decides to introduce herself to John, whom she knows will be working closely with her on the EduToy account. She stops by his office, notes he's typing on his computer, and says:

"Good morning John, my name is Marilyn Perkins. I just started last week as a marketing assistant, working on the EduToy account. I heard from my boss Carolyn that you're the creative lead for this client. I'd like to introduce myself—is this a good time?"

John says it is. After talking with John, she returns to her cubicle, stopping along the way to introduce herself to someone who sits a few desks down. She adjusts her opening lines accordingly:

> "Hi, my name is Marilyn Perkins. I'm new here, just started last week in marketing on the EduToy account. I'm not sure if we'll be working together, but since my desk is just over there I figure we'll be running into each other all the time. Is this a good time to say hi?"

The secret of a good opening is to keep it brief, respectful, and tailored to the prospective relationship. It's also wise to soften the intrusion by providing an "out" for the other person to delay the introduction to a better time.

The more you rehearse, reflect, and experiment with opening lines, the less anxious you'll be. Here's how one newcomer described her practice strategy:

> "I try to introduce myself more frequently. At work I will practice my introductions out loud, otherwise I will stutter. If I go by car to meet someone I will practice my introduction spiel, my one-minute spiel on why I'm there. It has helped, and you'd be shocked at how frequently I rehearse my introductions like how excited I am to be here and to create this relationship. That way I don't go into my nervous mode and start rambling."

SELF-INTRODUCTIONS: THE KEY TO SMALL (NOT REALLY) TALK

Sometimes after giving your opening lines, you quickly move into executing the new relationship (e.g., business meeting, service interaction, group event, consultation, etc.), but often the introduction is mostly just a few minutes of friendly small talk.

Recognize that this initial small talk isn't necessarily small or inconsequential. Through this initial conversation you start to establish and build your relationship with the other person, and the best, most effective conversations tend to help both parties in the following ways:

- You learn about each other.
- You explore what you already have in common (e.g., responsibilities, interests, acquaintances).
- You sense how you might interact in the future and what kind of future relationship you might have (e.g., teammate, office mate, neighbor, customer-client, friend, etc.).

There is no magic formula for what to discuss, and often you can't predict how the conversation will go. But typically most small talk during introductions tends to focus on the following things:

- Group and work roles
- Work and life histories
- Common interests and experiences
- Common acquaintances

Ideally, the conversation starts with something relevant to the context of your meeting and the relationship you're likely to develop. If you introduce yourself to someone at work, start the small talk around work roles and histories. If you introduce yourself to another parent at your daughter's soccer game, lead with small talk about your respective kids. If you introduce yourself to someone at a party, lead with how you are related to the host. Over time, you can drift into other, less context-relevant topics as you get to know each other.

SELF-INTRODUCTIONS: THE ART OF MAKING
A GOOD FIRST IMPRESSION

The secret to making a good first impression is to realize that it's not about wowing other people with your role, education, and/or accomplishments. Trying to do that will likely create a bad first impression, as you'll come off as a braggart and show-off.

Good first impressions are more about *how you make other people feel* during the introduction. Does interacting with you bring them energy? Do they leave the introduction feeling better about themselves? Do they get a chance to talk about themselves and impress you a little bit?

If you want to make a good first impression:

- Be humble.
- Be respectful.
- Be interested in them.

It sounds simple, but many newcomers I've interviewed say that, in the heat of the moment during introductions, they get nervous and either talk about themselves too much or talk about things that aren't interesting or don't energize the other person. They may also spend so much time worrying about what they'll say next that they aren't listening attentively to the other person (and it shows). Other times they might hesitate, stop talking, and let the conversation fall into an awkward silence.

When in Doubt, Ask Questions

One of the easiest and most reliable ways to make a good first impression is by asking questions. This includes asking questions about the other person's roles, background, and interests, as well as asking for information and advice about the organization.

Questions show your respect for and interest in the other person; also, people tend to gain energy from talking about themselves. If you ask for information and advice, people also get a chance to impress you with their experience and expertise, and they feel better about themselves if they can help others in some way. By asking questions you can also avoid talking too much about yourself, and you let the other people steer the conversation into areas they find interesting. Questions can also fill an awkward pause in the conversation if you both run out of things to say.

The key to success is to adopt a question-asking mindset whenever you introduce yourself to someone. Therapist and blogger Mark Tyrell states it nicely: "If I approach someone socially, I don't wonder what I'm going to talk about; I'm curious about what they're going to talk about.[6]

One newcomer I interviewed found that by focusing on the other person and asking questions, he actually reduced his own anxiety during introductions. He put it this way:

> "I assume everyone else is as uncomfortable as I am, and it's my duty to make them more comfortable, which helps me forget that I'm uncomfortable. I make them feel more comfortable by including them. I become the extrovert who is social and seemingly at ease but I'm not. It's my way of coping to forget that I'm awkward and uncomfortable."

If it helps, pretend you're a journalist whose job is to interview the people you want to meet. Adopting this mindset may make it easier to approach and interrupt someone, and keep you asking questions during the introduction. Obviously, you don't want to exhaust or annoy someone with too many questions, or say absolutely nothing about yourself, but usually most people will reciprocate your interest by asking a few questions of their own.

SELF-INTRODUCTIONS: THE CLOSING
AND CONTACT INFORMATION EXCHANGE

How long an introduction continues (or should continue) depends on a number of things:

- Availability and busyness of both parties
- How much you will likely interact with each other in the future (the more you know you'll be working closely together the more you'll probably spend time getting to know each other)
- How much energy you bring each other (the more you "click," the more you'll talk)

Generally, it's best to end the conversation while it still has energy and momentum, rather than letting it die out from a lack of good conversation topics or boredom. Let the other person drive the conversation's length, and look for signals he or she wants or needs to end the discussion. A timely exit shows respect for the other person's time.

As you conclude the introduction, remember to thank the person and express how much you enjoyed the conversation. If you think you might want to approach them later for help, advice, or more conversation, ask them. Most people will say yes to such an innocuous request, and you have them on record as willing to talk to you again. There are many ways to phrase an ending, depending on the situation:

"Great meeting you, Sarah. I really appreciate the conversation, and look forward to working with you on this project. If I have any more questions, do you mind if I stop by sometime?"

"Hey, I enjoyed this—nice to meet you! I look forward to talking some more at our kid's next soccer game . . . if that's all right with you."

If you'd like to exchange contact information, offer your own first. This sets up a reciprocal expectation that they'll give you their contact information, but gives them an "out" if they don't feel comfortable providing it.

WHAT TO DO AFTER THE INTRODUCTION

I can't emphasize this too strongly, but here goes:

WRITE IT DOWN!!!!

As soon as you can, write, type, or record on your smartphone everything you remember about the conversation—names, work roles, background, expertise, personal information, and any other interesting bits.

Most of us have really bad memories. You will quickly forget their names, or you will start to confuse their work and personal information with other people you've just met. You might think you'll remember all this stuff, but if you're normal, you won't. Trust me on this one.

For most of us it's very easy to blank on a name, confuse a person's role and background with somebody else's, or ask about something the other person already told us a few days ago. You'll save yourself a lot of anxiety and awkwardness if you can go back and refresh your memory before you meet the person again.

With clients and customers, and with some internal co-workers, you also might want to consider sending them a thank-you note or email. Thanking people for their time is another sign of respect, and more important it reinforces their memory of you, your role, and the potential of future interactions (because you know *they* probably didn't go back and write things down).

HOW TO REINTRODUCE YOURSELF

There are times when you will need to reintroduce yourself to others, including:

- When your initial introduction was really quick, or of poor quality (often by your busy boss) and didn't really establish any kind of relationship
- When the person seems familiar, but you can't recall whether you've ever been introduced to the individual before
- When the other person seems to be acting as if he or she doesn't remember your name or exactly who you are. The individual will appreciate the gesture.

It's not as embarrassing as you might think. Remember that almost everyone has a bad memory, and veterans know that newcomers have to meet and learn about lots of people. You can always lead with something like the following:

"Hi, I know we were introduced a couple weeks ago, but I just wanted to reintroduce myself. I'm Marilyn Perkins, over in marketing. I apologize, but it was such a whirlwind of introductions back then that I forgot your name."

"Hi, I've got a terrible memory, but I seem to recall we met a while back, maybe at a different company? I'm Marilyn Perkins—I just started a few weeks ago over in the marketing group, working on the EduToy account."

SELF VERSUS THIRD-PARTY INTRODUCTIONS

In most newcomer situations, the quickest, most effective approach is to introduce yourself. You have more control over the time and place of the introduction, and you're not imposing upon (or waiting on) someone else to make it happen. However, there are certain situations in which it might be wise to ask your boss, co-worker, or acquaintance to introduce you instead. For example:

- When that person can help you jumpstart an important, desired relationship by defining and publicly endorsing it, especially to the other person. For example, a boss might say, "John, let me introduce you to Marilyn, our new marketing assistant. You two will be working closely together to support the EduToy account, so I hope you'll take the time to really get to know one another."
- When that person can help establish your reputation and credibility with someone else. For example, a boss might say, "John, let me introduce you to Marilyn, our new marketing assistant. We just hired her away from our main competitor, and she knows all about designing effective marketing campaigns. She'll be a great asset on the EduToy account."
- When that person can help you gain access to a very busy, heavily scheduled individual.
- When the organizational or national culture clearly expects most introductions to go through third parties.

But remember that bosses, hosts, coaches, and teachers may be even more reluctant to introduce you to others than you are to introduce yourself. Not only do they end up assuming the social risk of approaching and interrupting other people, but sometimes they also risk the embarrassment of being expected to introduce you to people whose names they may not remember in the heat of the moment.

When You're the Third Party: Who Do You Introduce to Whom?

When you're new, you don't spend much time introducing other people, but the social uncertainty about who gets introduced to whom adds to the awkwardness of introductions. In most cultures, introductions typically are made so that the person of lower honor is introduced to the person of higher honor. The challenge is figuring out who is more "honored" in any particular situation. According to business etiquette books, the general direction is this:

- From a man to a woman
- From younger to older
- From lower rank to higher rank
- From fellow employee to customer or client
- From a peer in own company to a peer in another company
- From a nongovernment official to a government official

But even etiquette gurus admit that applying these rules in the modern workplace is often complicated and confusing. For example, suppose a forty-eight-year-old female is hired for an entry-level position at a high-tech startup and she meets the twenty-five-year-old male CEO. Who gets introduced to whom? The man to the woman? Youngest to oldest? The entry-level hire to the CEO? Nobody really knows which rule has priority, and as a result the guidelines have become less rigid (and even less well known) in the past few decades.

My advice is to be aware of these general guidelines, pick the direction that seems to be most appropriate, and then don't worry about it. As long as you show respect toward both parties in your introduction, it doesn't really matter much who gets introduced to whom these days, and few will take offense.

HOW TO REFLECT, PRACTICE, AND GET BETTER AT INTRODUCING YOURSELF

Introducing yourself to strangers is not hard in itself. The challenge is becoming more confident and comfortable at it so you don't hesitate or stay on the sidelines the next time you have the opportunity to do it. To get better at introducing yourself, you need to:

- Understand the source of your anxiety and reluctance
- Mindfully observe how you think, feel, and act when you introduce yourself
- Identify specific strategies to help you get better and more comfortable doing it
- Find opportunities to practice and experiment with new approaches

Examine Why You Are Reluctant

Think back to past situations in which you were nervous about approaching and introducing yourself to strangers. Did you hesitate because you:

- Didn't want to bother or interrupt what they were doing?
- Were worried about making a bad first impression?
- Didn't think you had a good enough reason to approach them?
- Weren't sure whether introducing yourself was socially appropriate?

Next, look for patterns to your anxiety and reluctance; for instance:

- Does your reluctance depend on the relative status of the other person (for example, bosses, experts, teachers, coaches)? If the person is male or female? Or of a different race or cultural background?
- Are you more reluctant to approach someone who is busy or who appears to be doing "important" work?

- Are there certain types of situations where you're more reluctant to introduce yourself? At work? At parties and mixers? At networking events? In classrooms?
- Are you more reluctant to introduce yourself to people you are likely to interact with in the future or to people you'll probably never see again?

Once you explore and understand where, when, and who you're most reluctant to introduce yourself, you can focus your observation and practice on those areas that will give you the greatest benefit.

Mindfully Observe How You Introduce Yourself

Over time all of us build up a set of assumptions, expectations, and habits surrounding self-introductions. By observing your thoughts, emotions, and behaviors as you approach and meet new people, you can uncover yours. This will help you identify the particular strategies that will help you get better and more confident when you are introducing yourself.

Over the next few days or weeks, make a commitment to pay attention to the self-introductions you make. As you approach the person, consider:

- Why you are introducing yourself
- What kind of relationship you will likely have with this person
- Whether you feel any reluctance about approaching and introducing yourself. If so, why?

As you introduce yourself and begin to have a conversation, try to momentarily "step outside yourself" and observe what you are thinking, saying, and feeling during the conversation. Consider the following questions:

1. Did your anxiety go away after the first few moments, or did it continue throughout the conversation? What does that tell you?

2. How were your opening lines? What was his or her reaction to your approach?

3. How did the small talk go? Did you explore common interests? Mutual relationships? Future interactions? What worked and what didn't?

4. Did the person seem to gain energy from the conversation? Did you talk too much or too little? Show interest in what the person said? Ask questions? Listen intently?

5. Did you end the conversation with either an explicit or implicit permission to approach the person again later? Thank him or her for their time? Write things down afterward?

6. Overall, how did the introduction go? Better or worse than you imagined it? Was your initial anxiety and reluctance justified?

After you feel you've observed yourself enough to generate some meaningful insights, review the strategies and approaches described in this chapter to determine which ones might help you get better at introducing yourself. Try them out to see if they make a difference.

Get Better Through Practice

Ultimately, the key to real improvement is creating opportunities to practice. If you worry about making a good first impression, start by introducing yourself to people where the social cost of making a mistake is low. If you are reluctant to bother busy people, introduce yourself to receptionists, retail clerks, waiters, librarians, nurses, and bank tellers—anyone who appears to be busy but probably has time for a brief introduction.

If you're uncomfortable approaching important people, practice introducing yourself to pilots, clergy, doctors, or teachers—anyone you think has higher status than you do. If these kinds of introductions feel really hard, pick people whom you're likely to never meet again. Does it really matter if you blow an introduction to a hotel receptionist or sales clerk while you're on vacation?

With all "practice" introductions, note other peoples' reactions. Did they yell at you? Throw you out? Call the police? In 99 percent of cases you'll find they'll reciprocate with at least their name, and you'll have a few seconds or minutes of pleasant conversation. See how little social risk there really is in introducing yourself to a stranger, and remember that fact the next time you're reluctant to approach someone. Practicing helps rewire your brain's natural tendency to overestimate the social cost of introductions.

If you aren't sure what to say during introductions, practice that. Create some opening lines and try them out with various people. Note their reaction and how well some specific opening lines lead to good conversations. Write out and rehearse the various elements of your work and life stories, and experiment with what you tell others. Note what facts and stories seem to generate energy in the conversation, and which ones make other peoples' eyes glaze over.

If you have a tendency to talk too much (or too little), create and memorize a list of standard questions you might ask to get people to talk about themselves. The next time you introduce yourself, practice asking people about their work, background, hobbies, and experiences. During the conversation, pay attention to how much time you are talking relative to the other person, and adjust accordingly. If you talk too much, force yourself to ask more questions. If you talk too little, force yourself to find opportunities to say something about yourself.

As you gain confidence in your ability to introduce yourself, start targeting people in your work and personal life whom you know you should introduce or reintroduce yourself to, such as:

- Key co-workers you haven't met yet (or met only briefly)
- New neighbors

- The person who sells you coffee every morning
- That familiar parent who is always standing next to you at school pickup
- Anyone to whom you've given a "smile and nod" more than once in the past month

Be patient, and keep practicing. Over time you'll get better and more confident at introducing yourself, and eventually you'll wonder why you were so stressed about it in the first place. More important, your life will be richer and more successful as a result of it.

SEVEN STEPS TOWARD SUCCESSFULLY INTRODUCING YOURSELF

1. Accept the awkwardness, but introduce yourself anyway.
2. Tailor your opening lines and initial conversation to the kind of relationship you expect to develop.
3. Create a good first impression by making the other person feel heard, valued, and respected, not by touting your own accomplishments.
4. Thank the individual for the conversation, and ask for permission to talk to that person later.
5. Write things down after the introduction.
6. Re-introduce yourself when necessary.
7. Practice, reflect, and practice some more.

SIX

REMEMBERING NAMES

In this chapter we will explore why most of us are bad at remembering names, and how to improve our ability to:

- Learn and memorize the names of new people
- Confidently recall people's names when we meet them again
- Avoid embarrassment when we don't

WHAT'S IN A NAME? EVERYTHING

Successful newcomers remember names. After the whirlwind of initial introductions, your ability to quickly and confidently recall peoples' names when you meet them again makes a big impact. It creates a very positive "second" impression. It surprises. It shows respect. It makes you look smart and competent. More important, it helps you jumpstart relationships and get what you need to be productive, accepted, comfortable, and happy in your new group.

Dale Carnegie once said, "A person's name is to that person the sweetest and most important sound in any language."[1] Babies learn to recognize and focus on their own names by the time they are five months old.[2] As adults, our brains react differently to the sound of our own name (versus other names),[3] even if we have severe brain damage and are in a persistent vegetative state.[4]

Famed psychologist Gordon W. Allport wrote that:

> The most important anchorage to our self-identity throughout life remains our name. . . . Our name is warm and central, a symbol of our whole being. How quickly we overhear it spoken in a room filled with conversing people. We feel offended if someone forgets it. . . . Here again we see that one's name, though only a symbol, is closely tied to one's self-esteem as it is to one's sense of self-identity.[5]

People are flattered when you remember their names, which creates something persuasion researchers call a "complimentary perception." In experiments these perceptions have led to greater compliance with requests and increased sales.[6] Scientists have even found that we subconsciously prefer words containing the letters of our own name, and even selectively pursue careers that sound like our own name (e.g., a disproportionate number of people named Dennis become dentists).[7]

Since we all intuitively understand that being able to quickly and confidently recall names is an important newcomer skill, why do most of us often:

- Forget a name soon after being introduced?
- Recall almost everything we've learned about a person *except* his or her name?
- Avoid situations where we might have to make introductions, because we fear we won't remember everyone's names?

When I ask newcomers to tell me how good they are at remembering names, they typically respond:

- "I'm terrible."
- "I'm really bad."
- "If I meet ten people and remember two or three of their names, I'll consider that a good day."

In the classroom, I sometimes ask my students to raise their hands if they consider themselves really good at remembering names. I've never seen more than three hands raised in a class of fifty. Then I ask students to raise their hands if they often forget a name within seconds of hearing it. Usually over 80 percent of the students laugh and raise their hands, and look relieved when most of their classmates have their hands up, too.

The problem with forgetting a name isn't so much that you forgot it; it's what you feel and do when you realize you can't recall it. Initially, most people feel shame and embarrassment. We wonder why we have such awful memories. More important, we often try to hide our ignorance from the other person, and that can ultimately hinder our ability to develop relationships and become a successful newcomer.

Our avoidance can be subtle, even subconscious. We smile and nod as we pass one another in the hallway, but pretend we're in a hurry and can't stop to chat. We give a friendly wave from afar, but avoid approaching the person. We might even adjust our intended path so we don't meet or quickly pull out and focus on our smartphone as if we just got an important message.

Ironically, by avoiding the situation, we actually miss out on what we want to happen if we could recall the person's name. In the perfect world of good memory, Sarah approaches and greets us by name; and we confidently respond with "Good Morning, Sarah!" In the glow of mutual recognition we both stop for a few minutes of friendly small talk. We might even get a chance to ask the newcomer a question or two.

Instead, in the real world of poor memory, Sarah approaches and greets us by name and we suddenly blank on hers. Then, we either reply with a sheepish "Hi!" or even worse, an over-the-top, fake "Hey, great to see you!" which doesn't hide our failure to remember her name and may actually draw attention to it. Either way, if we do stop to chat, instead of enjoying the experience and focusing on strengthening our mutual relationship we spend the entire conversation off balance, mentally trying to recall her name.

Ultimately, we leave the interaction feeling guilty and embarrassed, and even more reluctant to interact with her in the future, especially if we have no easy way of retrieving her name. Our reluctance to meet her will be exponentially greater if we are with a friend or colleague, when we will feel obligated (and expected) to make introductions.

In the end, all our blanking and avoiding just keeps us from building the relationships we need to be a successful newcomer. Fortunately, with a little understanding and a few techniques, we can reduce both of these problematic behaviors.

WHY IT'S SO HARD TO REMEMBER NAMES

When you're new, you know that you will introduce yourself (or be introduced) to many people. You know that during each introduction, you will hear the other person's name. You also know that you want to learn, recall, and say each person's name the next time you meet. You've had thousands of introductions to practice. So why are you so poor at it?

The fact is that failing to recall a name after an introduction is completely normal. Basically, our prehistoric brains are not hardwired to remember names well, and introductions are probably the worst time to hear, learn, and try to commit a name to memory. After all, the need to learn and recall individual names is a much more recent and uniquely human development, tied to the invention of complex spoken language. It's possible that we use older parts of our brain to process and store information about people, but have evolved a somewhat separate mechanism to process and store information about names.

Another potential reason for our difficulty remembering names is that for much of human history, we interacted with only a few dozen people at any one time, and almost never needed to rapidly learn many names at once, since it was never key to our survival. As a result, we never evolved the ability to do it well.

From a practical standpoint in today's environment, we fail to recall names because:

- We're distracted and don't pay enough attention to the name when we hear it, so it never gets into our short-term memory.
- Everything we learn about people right after their name keeps us from moving names from short- to long-term memory.
- Our brains process and store names differently from everything else we learn about people. Initially, the one-way neural connection between what we know about people and their names is very weak.
- Without mental effort, this one-way neural connection between face and name isn't strong enough to trigger recall of the name when we meet the person again.

However, once you understand why you are so bad at remembering names, you can take steps to ensure that you can consistently learn and retain people's names.

In One Ear and Out the Other

Imagine a typical introduction. Within the first few seconds you make eye contact, extend your hand, and say your name. The person reciprocates, and soon the sound waves of his or her name land on your eardrums, are converted into electrical signals, and are sent on to the brain for processing. So far, so good.

The brain processes the name (along with everything else you hear at the time) and puts it into echoic memory, where it remains for a few seconds (see Figure 6-1).[8] If you actively pay attention to the name while it is in this temporary storage area, it will likely end up in your short-term memory. If you don't, in a few seconds it's gone forever.[9]

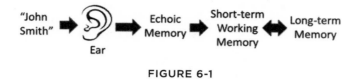

FIGURE 6-1

Test yourself the next time you make or receive an introduction. After you hear the person's name, wait a few seconds and mentally test your recall. If you've blanked on the name, you probably didn't pay enough attention to it while it was still in echoic memory.

What keeps you from paying attention? Everything else you think about when you're hearing a stranger's name. Your busy mind can be distracted by all sorts of parallel, competing thoughts:

- What do I say next?
- How am I connected to this person?
- How firm was my handshake?
- Is there food caught in my teeth?
- What are we having for lunch?
- Or whatever you were thinking about before the introduction

If you are in a noisy, crowded room, you may be distracted by other people's conversations. If you're being introduced to several people, you might be focusing on the next person (or still thinking about the last person). Sometimes your lack of attention is understandable, but often it is simply a bad habit. Over thousands of introductions, you've no doubt developed specific mental routines that you somewhat mindlessly perform when you make or receive introductions—for example, focusing on the handshake or what you plan to say.

Or, you might optimistically believe in your ability to mentally multitask, and assume that you can pay attention to the name and everything else you're thinking about at the moment. Either way, if your habits and assumptions don't include or reinforce a focus on the name, you've set yourself up for poor recall later.

Memories on Top of Memories

Even if you pay enough attention to the name to get it into your short-term memory, the next challenge is getting the name into long-term memory so it's there when you meet again.

Short-term memory is just as its name implies—a temporary storage system for both recently acquired memories and memories you've recently retrieved from long-term memory. Also known as *working memory*, this memory helps you think more swiftly and efficiently by giving your conscious mind quick access to the memories, information, and ideas you need *now*. While your brain is making use of short-term memories, it is also selectively processing and moving some of these memories into long-term memory through a largely subconscious process known as *consolidation*. Our brains don't have the capacity to remember absolutely everything we experience or think about, so the mind has evolved means to filter, combine, and store only a portion of our experiences.

This is where the problem of remembering names lies. If you pay attention to the name during the introduction, it may get into your short-term memory. But immediately after learning the name, you pay attention to and bring into short-term memory all sorts of other information about the person as well as miscellaneous thoughts and recalled memories that may occur during the introduction. This newer information interferes with the brain's ability to get a name into long-term memory.[10]

Test yourself. If you still remember a person's name a few seconds after hearing it, but can't recall it soon after the introduction, interference is likely the culprit.

The trick to overcoming interference is to develop a habit of repeatedly putting the name back into short-term memory during the introduction so it has a better chance of being consolidated into long-term memory.

The Crazy Way Names Are Processed and Stored

There is a third and more insidious reason you have trouble recalling names. Your brain actually processes and stores proper names like John Smith differently from how it does the other information you might learn about the person, including his face, occupation, family, likes, dislikes, and so on.[11] In general, your brain is relatively good at building neural connections between all of your memories *about* a person (see Figure 6-2). For example, seeing a person's face can trigger your recollection that he works in the marketing department, is married, and has three kids. Or that you first met him last Thursday.

Your brain is also relatively good at seeing or hearing people's names and then recalling information about them (see Figure 6-3). For example, if you meet and subsequently get an email from John Smith, you probably will be able to recall what he looks like and the odd fact that his favorite fruit is the kumquat.

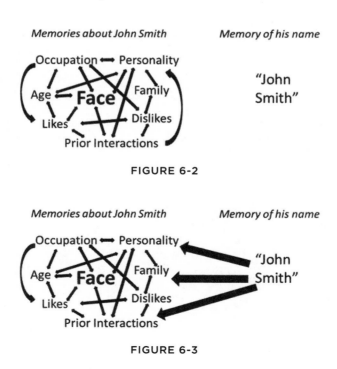

Memories about John Smith   *Memory of his name*

FIGURE 6-2

Memories about John Smith   *Memory of his name*

FIGURE 6-3

So why doesn't it work the other way around? Unfortunately, your brain is hardwired to be horrible at initially building a strong neural connection from what you know about a person to that person's name (see Figure 6-4). This is why you may unexpectedly meet someone, immediately recognize the face, and then discover you can recall everything about the person *except* his or her name.

Scientists call this phenomenon the *Baker-Baker paradox*. If we meet a man and learn that he is a baker, we often have no problem recalling that fact when we see him again. But if we meet a man and learn that his name is Baker, recalling it is much more difficult. The word is the same, but we process it quite differently.[12]

Have you ever felt as if you could almost recall a name, but mentally it was just out of reach? Scientists call this the *tip-of-the-tongue effect*; it turns out that this is much more common with people's names than with anything else you might try to learn and remember about a person.[13]

Last, modern technology is making the recall of names even more difficult. The inventions of email, instant messaging, and social media have made us lazy. Why learn and memorize peoples' names when every email, instant message, and Facebook post automatically includes the person's name? That's fine until you meet face to face, and discover that the neural pathways between what you know about a person and his or her name are still really, really weak.

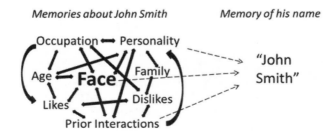

FIGURE 6-4

Fortunately, you're not doomed to blank on people's names forever. Each time you successfully recall a person's name, the neural pathways from information about that person to his or her name is strengthened. Once these connections are sufficiently strong, you can usually recall a person's name when you meet the individual again (see Figure 6-5).

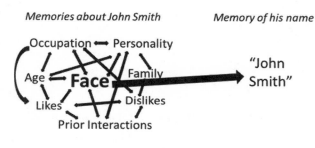

FIGURE 6-5

The "Fish Out of Water" Conundrum

Another reason you have trouble recalling names is that you have what scientists call *context-dependent recall*.[14]   Have you ever unexpectedly bumped into a co-worker, teacher, or doctor at the grocery store or shopping mall, and suddenly found you can't recall the person's name? You have no trouble remembering that name in the office, classroom, or hospital, but meet them somewhere other than the usual place and your mind goes blank. When we learn a name, we often incorporate the location and situation into our memory, and use that information as subtle cues to recall the name later. That approach works well until we meet them someplace where those situational cues aren't available.

STRATEGIES AND TECHNIQUES FOR LEARNING AND RECALLING NAMES

So there it is. Through a mixture of biology and bad habits, most of us are poor at learning and remembering names. We don't pay enough attention to names when we hear them. We keep them from getting into long-term memory by smothering names with all the additional information we hear and think about after the name. We process and store names differently from how we store other information about people, and initially we create a very weak link between faces and names. As a result, when we meet people again, we usually can recognize their faces and remember many things about them, but none of it automatically triggers recall of their names.

It Takes Practice: There Is No Free Lunch

None of the strategies and techniques I am about to discuss will quickly transform you into a memory savant who can meet people, hear their names once, and instantly recall their names forever.

Like all the other newcomer skills, it takes practice to see real improvement. Even after you've made these strategies and techniques a habit, you'll still go blank on names from time to time. But it'll happen less often, and you'll be better prepared to quickly recover and either recall or rediscover the name before it causes too much embarrassment.

Consistently Create a Strong Face-to-Name Connection

All of the following strategies and techniques for recalling names focus on one primary question: How can we consistently create a strong neural connection from our memories of people's faces to our memory of their names *before* we meet them again?

More specifically, how do we consistently create a strong connection between face and name when our brain is hardwired to process and store those two things differently? The solution is to develop the ability to learn and remember real or imagined things about people that give us clues to their names.

In a way, it's a form of cheating, or in IT terms, a "memory workaround." With this memory technique, you don't actually create a stronger neural connection between your memory of a person's face and your memory of that person's name. Instead, you create, learn, and store clues to the name in the same way you store memories of the face. Then, you take advantage of the fact that your brain is good at using memories about people to trigger other memories about people.

This way, when we recognize a face, it triggers memories of the clues that ultimately help us recall the differently stored name. Over time, through repeated recall, we strengthen the face-name link, and eventually we don't need the clues anymore.

Create Memorable Clues to People's Names

This strategy isn't new—in fact, it's the basis for almost every memory book ever written.[15] The objective is to create a clue (or set of clues) that (1) is consistently triggered when you see a face, and (2) helps you recall the name. Here are a few of the more popular techniques:

Turn the name into something silly and memorable and connect it to the face. I'm sure you've heard of this approach. For example, if you're trying to remember the following names, make the corresponding association:

- *Phillip Harper*: picture him trying to play a musical harp with his lips.
- *Sue Bartleman*: picture her in court suing Bart Simpson.
- *Rohit Singh*: picture him singing while he is rowing a boat.

The strategy is to:

- Make the imagery vivid, graphic, silly—the crazier, the better. Research has shown that sexually graphic imagery is remembered the best (so if you run into Harry Peterman, you know what to do).[16]
- Connect or incorporate the imagery into something about the person's face or physical appearance—a bushy eyebrow, mole on the

face, glasses, hair color or style, and so on. Use anything that helps trigger those crazy images when you meet the person again.

Connect the face to a memorable person with the same first or last name. A similar approach is to imagine the person standing next to or interacting with someone you already know who has the same first or last name. For example:

- *George Anderson*: picture him standing next to George Washington.
- *Sarah Gonzalez*: picture her with her arm around your high school teacher Mateo Gonzalez.

Mentally write the name on or above the face. A technique favored by Franklin D. Roosevelt was to imagine writing the name on the person's forehead.[17] Others imagine the person's name hovering over his or her head. Figure 6-6 illustrates how you might create some vivid imagery for the name John Smith that helps you recall his name when you see him again.

Regardless of the approach, connecting a person's face to a visual image works because you are making connections between memories that are processed and stored in similar ways. With experimentation and practice, you can get better and quicker at creating vivid and memorable clues to people's names.

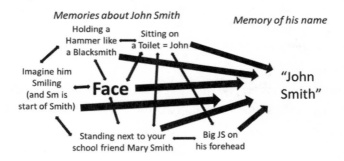

FIGURE 6-6

Of course, there are challenges with vivid imagery. Some names are hard to convert into vivid images. Some faces don't have memorable features that you can connect to imagined clues.

More important, without extensive practice, it can be really hard to use these techniques in the heat of the moment during introductions. Most of the time the conversation doesn't pause right after you hear the name, which leaves you trying to create a visual image while listening to the person and deciding what to say next. This approach also suffers from the same consolidation problem that names have: everything you learn about the person after you create your visual clues can prevent you from getting the clues into long-term memory.

Actually, the best time to use these techniques is before or after the introduction.

Learn Their Names Before You Meet Them

Why wait until the introduction to learn a person's name and face? In many newcomer situations, you can request a membership list or an organizational chart before you arrive. You can also search the Internet for names, pictures, and biographical descriptions.

Learning names (and ideally, faces) before you meet people offers several advantages. It gives you more time (and a less stressful environment) to study their names and create vivid, memorable clues, especially for hard-to-picture or foreign-sounding names. It gets the name into long-term memory before the introduction, so you can use your first meeting to create or strengthen the face-name connection. And it makes a great first impression if you can recognize and greet someone by name the first time you meet the individual.

Learn Names During Introductions

Unfortunately, most of the time your first opportunity to hear and learn a name is during the introduction, which is often the worst time to try to learn and memorize a name. So, rather than try to fully and permanently commit the name to long-term memory during the introduction, set a much more modest goal:

> *When you meet people, try to learn and remember their names long enough to write them down, so you can (1) commit the names to memory later and (2) remind yourself of the names if you forget.*

Once you've got their names on paper (or onto your computer or cellphone), learning and recalling those names becomes much easier. After the introduction, you can find a less stressful time to study and attach visual imagery of the names to your memory of their faces. You can repeatedly test your recall and strengthen the face-name connections.

More important, having names recorded in a known location can be a lifesaver if you forget a name. Your ability to recognize a correct name is much, much better than your ability to retrieve the name from long-term memory. Even people with brain damage who have completely lost the ability to recall the names of people they've just met can often recognize the names from a list of possible choices.[18]

To learn and remember names long enough so that you can write them down afterwards, make it a habit to:

- Remind yourself to pay attention to names.
- Repeat names immediately after hearing them.
- Use them during the ensuing conversation.
- Study faces and note any distinctive features.
- Mentally test your recall of their name several times during the introduction.
- Get their names on paper or onto your cellphone during or immediately after the introduction.

Make a mental commitment to listen for and learn names. As soon as you realize you are about to make or receive an introduction, make a mental commitment to listen for, pay attention to, and learn names. One newcomer told me that before he meets people, he'll say to himself "Remember their name, remember their name." If you make focusing on names part of your "mental checklist" for all introductions, you will more likely be paying attention to the name when you hear it.

Repeat names immediately after hearing them. Your first objective is to properly hear the name and pay it enough attention to get it from echoic to short-term memory. Making it a habit to repeat a person's name immediately after hearing it can ensure your recall will last more than a few seconds.

There are a number of ways that you could repeat and maintain focus on a person's first name, such as:

- "Hi, John, nice to meet you."
- "Srinivasan, did I say your name correctly?"
- "Linda, is that spelled L-i-n-d-a or L-y-n-d-a?"
- "Kate, is that short for Katherine?"

Similarly, for the last name you could say:

- "Pallatino, did I say that correctly?"
- "Bourque—how do you spell that?"
- "Patterson—are you related to the Jon Patterson who works down at the hardware store?"

It matters less how you focus on the name than that you make it a habit to do so. Most people are flattered if you show interest in their names. If it ends up feeling awkward, you can always say you like to repeat a name so you can learn it better.

Use the name during and especially at the end of the ensuing conversation. Once the name exchange is over and you continue hearing and processing even more information about the person, all that newer information can prevent you from getting the name into long-term memory. To counter this, make it a habit to use names during the ensuing conversation.

Obviously, you don't want to repeat names so much that you sound goofy, but habitually using names once or twice during a conversation can help improve later recall. How you do it is up to you, and it will vary from introduction to introduction:

- "So, Ernestine, where do you work?"
- "I'm curious, Paul, what do you think about our new mayor?"
- "How long have you been here at Pinnacle, Bart?"

One of the most critical moments to repeat a name is at the end of the introduction. This brings the name back into short-term memory and ensures that the name is one of the last things your brain processes before ending the conversation. This increases the probability that you will remember the name long enough to write it down soon afterwards.

It's also nice to repeat your own name at the end of the introduction. Since most people are bad with names, and have likely forgotten yours already, repeating your name can generate lots of goodwill. If you've forgotten the person's name, repeating your own can prompt them to repeat their name as well. There are many ways to do this:

- "Nice to meet you, Jason—thanks for the introduction. Once again, I'm Phil."
- "And your name again was Connor, right? I'm Miguel."
- "Corbin, it's been a pleasure meeting you. In case you didn't catch it earlier, I'm Jerry."
- "Carolyn, I look forward to meeting you next week. And again, I'm Mary. "
- "Great to meet you! Once again, my name is Amit, and yours again was . . . ?"

Study the person's appearance, especially the face. Your ultimate objective is to ensure that when you see people again, their faces consistently trigger recall of their names. This requires that you not only make it a habit to learn their names, but also that you make it a habit to "learn" their face and general appearance. Focus on distinctive features that you can associate with their name, such as:

- Shape of head, nose, lips, ears
- Head and facial hair (hair, eyebrows, sideburns, mustache, beards)
- Eye color and spacing, eyeglasses (if worn)
- Height and weight
- Posture and walk

As with names, the challenge during introductions is to make a commitment to really look at and study the person while you are engaging in a conversation. Some of us tend not to maintain eye contact, and we stare at the floor instead of the person we're talking to; as a result, we end up walking away with only a vague sense of what the person really looked like.

Test Yourself. One of the most beneficial things you can do during an introduction is to mentally quiz yourself on people's names while you are talking to them. Just look at their faces and try to recall their names. Was it instantaneous and easy? Or, did you have to think about it a while? Have you forgotten it already? Not only does testing yourself confirm that you have their names in short-term memory, but also the repetition helps strengthen the overall neural connection between faces and names. If you've already forgotten the name, you can ask for it again at the end of the introduction.

The Value of Business Cards, Pictures, and Videos

Obviously, if you can walk away from the introduction with a record of the person's name, you're golden. Sometimes you can exchange business cards. You can also pull out pen and paper and say something like "I don't want to forget your name. Let me write it down right away." If you're bold, you can do something like pull out your smartphone and ask if you can videotape the person saying his or her name, which will help you to firmly connect faces to names.

AFTER THE INTRODUCTION

Once the introduction ends, the real work of learning and memorizing a name begins. Focused study and testing yourself is the key to ensuring that you'll remember people's names later, especially in the heat of the moment.

Make a Record of the Name

Don't trust your memory. As soon as you can after meeting someone, record the name where you can find it later. If you have the time, include some notes about the person. There are many ways to do this:

- *Notebook or day calendar.* I carry a small leather-bound note-book in my back pocket, primarily for names. In a pinch, write the name down on anything—reports, memos, receipts, nap-kins, or any handy piece of paper. For some people, the physical act of writing down a name helps get the name into long-term memory.
- *Smartphone.* Type the name into a notepad application. Make a voice recording. Videotape yourself saying the name. Create a new contact in your email software.

- *Email record.* Send the name to yourself—or better yet, send the other person an email acknowledging the meeting. Emails are particularly good because they are inherently searchable, and they provide a permanent timestamp of your initial meeting. With our crazy brains, it's often easier to remember when you met a person than what the person's name is.
- *Computer contacts list.* Type the name into your computer, ideally into a document in which you consistently record the names of people you meet.

How and where you record the name is less important than doing it as soon as possible after the introduction. Your ability to find and recognize a name you've written down is often much easier than your ability to recall a name you've only heard once or twice.

Find Time to Study, Learn, and Test Your Recall

The only way you'll consistently and confidently recall names is by studying and learning the names of people you've met before you meet them again. The imagery techniques work pretty well, but only if you put in the additional effort. Just relying on what you accomplished during the introduction is often not enough.

Here are some ways to practice:

1. *The Walking Quiz.* Take a stroll around your new surroundings, looking at people and trying to recall their names. If the name comes easily, move on. If you blank on the name, study the face and appearance a bit more. Later, review your lists and try to connect it with the name. Repeat the vivid imagery techniques, and test yourself again later.
2. *The Photo Quiz.* If you have access to photos of people you've met (either pictures you've taken, or on websites, or elsewhere), test

yourself by looking at the pictures and trying to recall their names.

3. *Names Lists Review*. Periodically review your lists of names. Study a name, and try to picture the person in your mind, along with anything else you can remember about the person. Try to recall the vivid imagery you used when you first learned the name, or come up with new imagery. Your goal is to reinforce the neural pathways between information about people and their names so you can recall their names later.

4. *Flashcards*. One technique I use to learn the names of students is to create flashcards with photos and names on them. I periodically go through the flashcards, testing myself by looking at the pictures and trying to recall the names. If I recall the name quickly and easily, I put it into the "quick recall" pile. If I don't, I put it in the "slow or failed recall" pile. When I've gone through all the cards, I return to the "slow or failed" cards and try to re-learn the names using visual imagery techniques, and then I test myself again. I judge progress as a growing stack of "quick recall" cards, and a shrinking stack of "slow or failed recall" cards.

You'll find that some names go effortlessly into memory, and that you have no problem remembering them weeks, months, and perhaps years later. Others will be more stubborn and resist all attempts at recall, despite your best efforts to learn and re-learn the names. Be patient.

PRIME YOURSELF BEFORE YOU MEET AGAIN

You can dramatically improve your ability to recall names if you review people's names and faces just *before* you interact with them again. Memory researchers call this *priming*. By doing it, you activate and temporarily energize the neural pathways between information about the person and his or her name, increasing the chances your brain will make the connection when you see the person again.[19]

Over time, as the neural pathways are reinforced and your ability to recall the name becomes easier, the value of priming diminishes.

What to Do if You Forget a Name

Face it; despite all your best efforts to learn people's names, you're going to blank on somebody, even people you've known for years. Depending on the situation, there are several things you can do:

- *Be the Newcomer*. If you're still new, relax. No one expects you to remember everyone's name, so you can often just reintroduce yourself without much social penalty. When you're new, you often have to learn and remember many names, while the old-timers have to learn and remember just one name—yours.

  You can admit you have forgotten the name, and say something like "I'm sorry, I met so many people over the past few days I've forgotten your name. I'm Karen, by the way." Or, you can reintroduce yourself and give your name, such as "Hi, we met briefly last week, but I'd like to reintroduce myself—my name is Karen." The person will likely reciprocate by repeating her or his own name, and probably will be relieved (since the person likely will have forgotten your name, too).

- *Be the Detective*. In some situations, you have the time and social space to try to figure out peoples' names before you need to say them. Remember that you are much more likely to recognize the correct name than to pull it out of memory. There are a number of ways to make this happen:
  - Review your lists of names. That's another reason to carry the lists with you.

- Look through organizational charts, websites, anywhere you think the name might be. Since you're more likely to remember information about a person than his or her name, that information can help narrow your search for the name.

- Do a Google search for information you know about a person; this can generate the name. For example, if you knew the person ran a charity 10k in a neighboring town last month, you can review the race results list and see if you recognize the name.

- Look through old emails. If you've interacted with people via email, you can often search by keyword for something you know about them (such as a project, organization, or day and time you met) and then review the sender names.

- Go through the alphabet in your head and think of potential names that start with that letter. Sometimes that will trigger the name.

- Ask someone. For most people, it's less embarrassing to ask a third party for another person's name than to admit to someone you've forgotten his or her name. Even if the person you ask doesn't know the name, the individual might know something else about the person that can help your detective work.

- *Be Sneaky.* Sometimes you can avoid embarrassment by less direct means:

  - Eavesdrop on conversations between the person and other people. Often you'll hear someone speak his or her name, either as a greeting or during an introduction.

  - Conspire with a friend. Sometimes you're in the worst-case scenario where it appears you will have to introduce a friend to someone whose name you've already forgotten. Before you approach, ask your friend to proactively make a self-introduction. The other person will usually reciprocate with his or her name. Problem solved!

- *Be Human*. Often the simplest and most expedient solution is to admit that you have a bad memory and have momentarily "blanked" on the name. Sometimes you can use information you remember about people to show that you haven't completely forgotten who they are, but just can't recall their names.
    - "I'm sorry; I can't believe that I've just blanked on your name. Sometimes I have a horrible memory and can't even remember my kids' names."
    - "I'm sorry; I've forgotten your name. Sometimes when I haven't talked with someone in a while the name just flies out of my head."
    - "I'm sorry; I've just blanked on your name. I know you live over on Elm Street and your son Tim is in my daughter's class, but for some reason I just can't recall your name right now."

Remember that most people have bad memories and will understand when you can't recall their names. In some situations, they'll be surprised that you knew it in the first place. What often matters more is the respect and humility you show to them after you admit you've forgotten their name.

HOW TO REFLECT, PRACTICE, AND GET BETTER AT REMEMBERING NAMES

The good news is that almost everyone can get better at remembering names. To get there you need to:

- Reflect on why, where, and in what kinds of situations you blank on names.
- Mindfully observe how you currently hear, learn, and recall names.

- Identify strategies to more consistently learn names before, during, and after introductions.
- Find opportunities to practice.

Explore Why, When, and Where
You Have Trouble with Names

Think back to past situations when you've suddenly blanked on people's names. Why do you think they occurred? Is it because you were:

- Not paying enough attention to names when you first heard them?
- Not making an active attempt to get the names into long-term memory, either during or after the introduction?
- Not reinforcing your memory of the names through review and "priming" before you met the person again?

Next, look to see if there are patterns to what you forget. For example, does your memory vary based on the:

- Type of name? Are you more likely to blank on common names? Unusual names? Foreign-sounding names?
- Likelihood of meeting the person again? Do you pay less attention to the names of people you don't think you'll interact with in the future?
- Importance you attach to remembering that person's name? Do you tend to focus less on names of people you deem "less important" to your future success?
- Number of people you meet at the same time? Are you overwhelmed when you are introduced to too many people at once?
- Context of the introduction? Are you more likely to blank on the names of people you meet at work? Parties? Networking events? Organizing meetings? Random encounters?

- Context of the meeting? Do you tend to blank on names of people you suddenly meet in an unusual place? Or in situations where you have little time for recall?

The more you understand about why, when, and where you blank on names, the easier it will be to choose the right strategies and approaches to improve your ability to remember names.

Mindfully Observe How You Currently Learn Names

The next step to diagnosing and improving your ability to recall names is to examine how you currently pay attention to, learn, and commit names to memory. Reflecting on the past isn't enough, however; you need to analyze how you actually think and act during introductions to fully uncover the reasons you sometimes fail to remember names. Only then can you select and practice the strategies that will allow you to more consistently and confidently recall names in the heat of the moment.

Over the next few days or weeks, make a commitment to observe how you think about names when meeting new people. A few seconds after you hear a person's name, mentally try to recall it. If you can't, try to diagnose why you weren't paying enough attention to it. Were you focused on some other aspect of the introduction—say, the handshake? What to say next? Were you distracted by other people or room noise? If you can recall only a part of the name (such as the beginning or ending sounds, its relative length, number of syllables, etc.), make a note of that, too. What does that tell you about your memory?

If you do recall the name, let the conversation continue for a few more minutes and test your memory again. If you've forgotten it, again try to diagnose why that happened. Do you feel as if the person's name has been "covered up" by new information? What do you recall about the person? Is the name on the "tip of your tongue" or lost completely? Do you remember part of the name; if so, what part?

Once you've concluded the conversation and parted ways, wait a few minutes and test your recall not only of the person's name but also of his or her face and any other identifying characteristics. Does your memory of the name feel "solid" in your mind, is somewhat tentative, or have you forgotten all or part of the name? Can you picture the person's face well enough to describe it to a police sketch artist? If not, what's missing from your memory?

Finally, make a commitment to test your recall the next day, and see how well you do. Repeat this process with a few other introductions, and see if you notice any patterns, processes, or habits that impact your ability to learn and recall a name. Review the strategies described earlier in this chapter and see which ones might help you more consistently pay attention to, learn, and recall names when you need them. Try them out and see if they make a difference.

Find Opportunities to Practice and Experiment

Memory researchers have shown that most people can get better at learning and remembering names if they practice the listening, repetition, and vivid imagery techniques. The goal is not only to master these techniques but, more important, to make them a habit so you consistently use them during introductions. Here are some ways to practice:

- *Introduce yourself to random people*—retail clerks, librarians, wait staff, mail carriers, flight attendants, and the like. Practice listening for the name, repeating it right away, and using it during the conversation. Test yourself a few seconds and a few minutes after the introduction. Experiment with different imagery techniques and various ways to write down or record the name after the conversation.

- *Practice imaginary introductions.* Pick people who you don't know out of a magazine or website. Pretend you're meeting them, and use imagery techniques to learn their names. Conduct a pretend conversation with them, and practice listening, repeating, and using their names. Test yourself seconds or minutes later to see if you can recall their names.

- *Use memory practice websites.* For example, Lumosity[20] offers a suite of games and exercises to improve memory, including face-name recall. In one game you play the role of a waiter who has to remember the faces, names, and orders of customers.

If your challenge is paying attention to the name the first time you hear it, anticipate and focus on the name to the exclusion of everything else, and then test your recall. If your challenge is keeping the name in your head long enough to write it down, focus on consistently testing your recall throughout the conversation, and remind yourself to use vivid imagery techniques. If your challenge is long-term recall, focus on writing names down and developing routines to review, test, and "prime" yourself for future interactions.

The more you practice these techniques, the more effective and easier they will become.

SIX STEPS TO SUCCESSFULLY REMEMBERING NAMES

We often have trouble recalling names, but you can get better at it by:

1. Relaxing. Most of us are bad with names.
2. Committing yourself to pay attention to the name before you meet someone new.
3. Repeating the name once you've heard it and using it during the introduction to ensure you've stored it in your short-term memory. Mentally test your recall to make sure it's there.
4. Writing the name down as soon as you can.
5. Using vivid imagery techniques (during the introduction, if possible, and especially afterwards). Periodically test your recall

ability, and "prime" yourself by reviewing names prior to meeting people again.

6. If you forget a name, you can re-introduce yourself, search through your lists and files to help you recall the name, or simply apologize for forgetting and ask again.

SEVEN

ASKING QUESTIONS

In this chapter we will explore why, when we're new, we are sometimes reluctant to ask questions, and we'll learn how we can improve our ability to:

- Be more strategic and proactive in asking questions.
- Approach others and ask questions with less anxiety.
- Ask questions in ways that create or maintain a positive impression.

We all know that asking questions is often the only way we can receive the help, information, or advice we need to get up to speed quickly and become a successful newcomer. When we're new, we need others to help us filter the fire hose of new information we're receiving. We need feedback on how we're doing and advice on what really matters. When we become leaders, most of what we achieve is through others, and success requires us to ask questions and make requests to dozens of people across the organization and beyond.

Sure, we can find some of what we need on the Internet. But much of the really important, useful stuff is only found inside the heads of experts, teachers, coaches, salespersons, co-workers, neighbors, and others who simply have more experience with the situation than we do.

Research shows that the more questions newcomers ask and the more help they seek, the better they tend to perform at work; in addition, co-workers see them as more creative. Question-askers are also more satisfied in their new jobs and more committed to their new group and organization.[1] Students who ask more questions also tend to get better grades.[2] But despite all the benefits that come from asking questions, we sometimes find ourselves:

- Wasting time searching for information using Google instead of just walking down the hall, or picking up the phone, or raising our hand, or turning to the person sitting or standing next to us
- Spending more effort *worrying* about asking someone a question than actually doing it
- Leaving a store, restaurant, or doctor's office regretting that we didn't ask any questions

I usually end interviews with the question: "If you could go back in time and be new again, what would you do differently?" By far the most common answer is: "Ask more questions."

When I ask newcomers why they don't ask more questions, the most typical responses I get are:

"I didn't realize what others knew."
"I was reluctant to approach and bother other people."
"I felt I needed to figure it out by myself."

One newcomer described it this way:

"I was a little chagrined. Do you remember the old movie *My Cousin Vinny*? When Joe Pesci, the bumbling lawyer, said that if only he could see what information the prosecution had, the judge said 'Don't you know that you can ask for all of it?' It was a little like that. I hadn't thought to ask, or didn't realize that others could give me that stuff. I was reluctant to ask for it, or felt I could find it on my own."

Reluctance to ask questions affects even the best and brightest. I interviewed an engineer who graduated with honors from Stanford University. During her first job after graduation she told me:

"I was terrified to ask people questions. I was afraid of seeming dumb. I don't think that was a good approach because I spent a lot of time trying to learn something that someone could have told me in a few minutes."

MIT researcher Tom Allen interviewed one newcomer who put it this way:

"I think people, being human, are somewhat reluctant to go to a person that they don't know. Either you are afraid you are going to look like a "schnook" when it's all over or you are afraid that this guy may not have enough time. I think everybody goes through this ever since they were kids."[3]

In hindsight, many can point to situations in which their reluctance had a huge impact on their performance. For example, one person I interviewed started a new job as a computer programmer. During his first project he discovered he needed to combine two large segments of computer code. Rather than ask his cubicle neighbors how he might accomplish this task, he dove into the challenge, working by himself for over two weeks to manually combine the two segments. After he was done, he found out that months earlier the company had purchased a software tool that could have combined the two segments in minutes. Ouch!

Sadly, our reluctance to ask questions can sometimes feed on itself. If we don't ask questions, we often find ourselves lacking critical information, and that uncertainty makes us anxious, which makes us even more reluctant to ask questions. But with a little understanding about why we're sometimes reluctant to ask questions, and a few techniques and practice strategies, we can become more comfortable and confident doing it.

WHY THE RELUCTANCE TO ASK QUESTIONS?

The reasons we avoid asking questions when we're new are similar to why we fear introducing ourselves. Once again, our reluctance to ask questions is thousands of years in the making. In prehistoric times, doing something to reveal our relative lack of knowledge and expertise within the group could lead to a reduction in our status and even outright rejection. As a result, we developed a natural reluctance to expose our ignorance to others.

For most of human history, our relative knowledge and expertise were demonstrated by *what we did*. But once we developed language, it was also revealed by *what we said*, including the questions we asked. These days, we often don't think of our interactions with others as status competitions, but when we approach others to ask questions, that ancient fear of losing group status kicks in.

As children, we also *learn* to be reluctant through our interactions with parents, teachers, and classmates.[4] At first our questions are welcomed as cute and adorable, but over time we discover that questions can also be annoying or awkward. We also learn that there are times when it's not a good idea to ask a question. We're also told *never* talk to strangers, which makes it hard for us as adults to ask questions of unfamiliar people.

At school, we are told to *raise our hands*, wait to be called on, and to ask our questions *in front of the entire class*. No pressure there! We quickly discover that questions reveal a great deal about fellow students. For instance, was it a good question? Or, was it a slacker question from someone who didn't do the homework? Or, a naïve question from someone who doesn't really understand the big picture? Or, a suck-up question from someone wanting to impress the teacher? Or, a know-it-all question from someone trying to prove he's the smartest kid in the room? No wonder many of us graduate with a general reluctance to ask questions.

Overall, the competitive, compare-myself-to-others aspects of modern education may have taught many of us to be more reluctant to ask questions than we need to be. Education researchers Alison Ryan, Lynley Hicks, and Carol Hidgley studied a group of 443 fifth-graders.[5] They found that students who were mostly focused on *performing well* relative to their fellow students tended to be much more reluctant to ask questions than those who were oriented toward *learning and improving*. When we see every question we ask as a "reveal" of our competence and ability, we're much more anxious about asking them.

The Internet has added a new wrinkle. It is a phenomenal resource, and now much of the information we want or need is only a search engine and a few clicks away. But its blessing (and curse) is that it also allows us to get information without the awkwardness of having to physically approach and ask other people, especially strangers, questions.

For example, with Google Maps, MapQuest, and GPS, we never have to stop and ask for directions. With Yelp and Trip Advisor, we don't have to ask hotel staff and other strangers for restaurant recommendations. With home-improvement YouTube videos, we never have to admit to the hardware-store employee that we don't have a clue how to re-tile our bathroom floor. Even if we do have to ask a question online, it usually is more anonymous and less stressful than approaching someone face to face.

The problem arises when we:

- Think we always need to do an exhaustive search on the Internet *before* we earn the right to ask a question.
- Assume it's inappropriate to ask a question that we *might* be able to answer through an Internet search.
- Always go to the Internet first, even when we know it might be the worst place to quickly get what we need.

More important, if we get most of our answers via Internet searches, we don't get the practice and reflection we need to recalibrate our brain and become more comfortable asking questions face-to-face.

Three Questions We Ask When We Think about Asking

Our reluctance to ask questions is often based on three questions we subconsciously ask ourselves when we consider asking someone a question:

1. Is It Appropriate to Ask This Person This Question Right Now?
The purpose of this question is to evaluate whether asking *this particular question* to *this particular person* violates any prevailing social norms. In general, we tend to be more reluctant to ask questions of *higher status* people: bosses, teachers, coaches, experts, respected people like doctors or priests, and famous people. There is an implicit social assumption that their time is more valuable than ours, so we ask ourselves if, by bothering them with this particular question, we are somehow "breaking the rules." For instance, you wouldn't seek out your CEO to ask directions to the bathroom.

We also tend to avoid asking questions of *busy people*. Asking a question when someone is clearly focused on something else represents a greater imposition than if that person were standing idly by the water cooler. Since higher status people are often very busy, we can be doubly reluctant to ask a question. Here's how one newcomer described it:

> "I'm a bit frustrated. . . . Everyone's busy, so I can't go and ask the questions that I want to ask. Tim was out for a while and now he's talking with some marketing people and Sundar is talking to someone also. I've gotten to a point where I really need some clarification to proceed. So, I'm fuddling around with my account to get some new software to run on it, which is a reasonable thing to do, but not what I want to be doing."

2. What Will the Person Think of Me if I Ask This Particular Question Right Now?

This question is about how the person you ask will evaluate your competence and intent. Will the question make you look intelligent or incompetent? Savvy or naïve? Expert or beginner? This fear increases the more you value making and maintaining a positive impression on the other person.

We also assume that the longer we're in a new situation, the more we're expected to know. Here's how one newcomer put it:

> "I was somewhat afraid that I was going to ask dumb questions—I think the longer I have been here the more I think I should know about everything, even things not related to my project."

Researchers have shown that *males* in particular are more reluctant to ask questions and seek help than females,[6] especially when they:

- Feel they are in a competitive environment.
- Might reveal ignorance in an area traditionally associated with being male.

- Might violate expectations that males should be self-reliant and "in control."

3. What Will I Think of Me if I Ask This Person This Question Right Now?

Sometimes this is the most reluctance-producing question of all. It's often hard for us to accept that we don't know as much as we think we do, or that we're more of a beginner than we care to admit. If you find yourself reluctant to ask a question of someone you'll likely never meet again, you're probably more worried about damaging your own ego than the long-term social risk of asking.

Overestimating the Possibility of "No"

A lot of our reluctance to approach others with questions comes from assuming that we're asking for help, information, and advice without providing much in return. We use up the other person's time and effort, and all that person gets back (at least initially) is our gratitude. We imagine all the hassle and aggravation our interruption will create, and all the good reasons the person has for saying no. We fear the inevitable rejection and dismissal we'll likely get if we impose our questions upon others, especially strangers.

But researchers Frank Flynn and Vanessa Bohns have found that we tend to overestimate the probability that other people will say no to our requests.[7] In one study, they asked a group of undergraduate students to predict how many strangers they would have to ask in order to get five to complete a questionnaire. On average, students thought they'd need to ask over twenty people to meet their five-survey quota. In reality, they needed to ask only about ten. They found the same thing when they asked students to predict how many strangers they'd need to ask to borrow a cellphone (ten predicted, six actual) or get an escort across campus to the college gym (seven predicted, two actual).

But do people overestimate the no's in *real* situations? The researchers collaborated with the nonprofit organization Team in Training to find out. Team in Training raises money for leukemia research by helping athletes train for endurance events like marathons and triathlons. In exchange, the athletes agree to raise a minimum amount of money ($2,100 to $5,000 depending on the race).

Flynn and Bohns asked the athletes to predict how many people they would need to ask in order to reach their fundraising goal. On average, the athletes predicted they would have to ask 210 people, but in reality they needed to ask only 122 people. Even athletes who had raised money the year before significantly overestimated how many people would say no to their sponsorship requests.

As the researchers explored why people might consistently overestimate the probability that others would say no, they found that when we think about asking other people for a favor, we mostly focus on how much of an imposition the request might be and all the reasons why the other person might say no. But we rarely put ourselves in the other person's shoes and think about how hard it might actually be to *politely refuse* a reasonable request, and all the benefits that come from *answering* questions.

Most people want to be seen as (and see themselves as) a helpful person who is valued for his or her knowledge and expertise. One way we can demonstrate that helpfulness and expertise is by accepting requests and answering questions. Think back to the last time someone stopped you on the street and asked for directions. Was your first impulse to say no, or did you automatically try to help? Did you walk away feeling annoyed, or did you come away with a warm fuzzy feeling that you're "that kind of person" who helps others?

One newcomer I interviewed put the benefit this way: "I've learned that people love to be asked questions. Many see it as a compliment."

So, when you find yourself reluctant to ask someone a question, try putting yourself in that person's situation. Ask yourself: "If I had that person's role, position, and knowledge, and a new person came up and asked me a question, what would I think and do?" If your typical reaction would be to stop what you're doing and answer the question, and you consider yourself normal, *why would you think the other person would react any differently?*

STRATEGIES THAT MAKE ASKING QUESTIONS EASIER

Don't let your reluctance stop you from getting the information, help, and advice you need to be a successful newcomer. Remember that you often stand more to lose from not asking the question. As one purported Chinese proverb puts it:

> *He who asks a question is a fool for five minutes; he who does not ask a question remains a fool forever.*[8]

Advance Preparation: Build a Relationship

Often the easiest way to reduce your reluctance is to first introduce yourself and build a friendly, positive relationship with people *before* you need to ask them a question. The more people you get to know, the more options you have to get your questions answered. It's also hard for your question to create a bad first impression if it's the second, third, or tenth time you're interacting with someone.

Introductions are also a great time to find out what people know and to judge how receptive the individual might be to your future questions. During the introduction, you can also ask for *advance* permission to ask questions later. If you say something like "Would you mind if I stop by sometime if I have a question?" most people will say yes to such an innocuous request. This gives you justification for approaching the person later, and it also makes it harder for the person to refuse your request when you do.

Consider Your Mindset: What You Want and Why

Ask yourself what you are really trying to accomplish by asking someone a question. Do you want information, advice, feedback, assistance, reassurance, or permission? Are you asking for a few minutes of the person's time, or something more? Does he or she have to make a decision to provide you an answer? The clearer you can be about what you want, the easier it will be to ask the question and the greater the likelihood your request will be understood and you will receive a useful answer.

Is it possible to ask dumb or inappropriate questions that make you look bad? Of course. Anyone who tells you that "there is no such thing as a dumb question" is lying to you. But the fastest way to ask a dumb question is to use a mindless process to create the question in the first place.

It also turns out that your mindset *about* asking questions makes a difference. Researchers Dvora Geller and Peter Bamberger studied a group of 110 new customer-service agents at an Israeli telecommunications company.[9] They found that question-asking didn't automatically lead to higher performance. What mattered was the mindset that newcomers had *about* asking questions. If they mostly approached others with questions in order to *learn* how to do their job more effectively, more questions led to higher performance. But if newcomers asked questions simply to get others to help them do their work, more questions didn't lead to better performance.

In other words, when it comes to questions, a "teach me" mindset is generally more effective than a "tell me" mindset. Put a third way, asking others to "help me learn to solve my own problem" works better than asking others to "solve my problem."

Before Asking, Do Your Homework

Obviously, you don't want to bother busy people with questions that Google or a quick search of organizational websites and databases might uncover. Sometimes the act of searching for an answer on the Internet can also help you refine and improve your question. Still, you don't want to waste your own valuable time searching endlessly for information you can get quickly from others.

A good rule of thumb is to search for the answer *for only as long as you need to convince yourself that the answer is not obvious and the question you're asking makes sense*. If you are worried about asking a dumb question, think of it this way: the Internet now contains about every kind of dumb question ever asked. So if you can't find it right away, then it's probably not a dumb question.

Consider the law of diminishing returns when it comes to research. Once it's clear that the answer is not obvious, the chances that the next search results page, website, report, or archived email will reveal the answer is very low. At that point, you're better off asking someone the question.

Three Things to Consider when Determining Whom to Ask

Once you realize you need information, help, and advice, who should you ask first? Sometimes there is only one clear choice, but often you have some control over who you initially approach with your question. There are three things you might consider when deciding who to ask:

Who Might Be Helpful?
Obviously, you want to ask someone you think knows the answer. Depending on the question, it could be a manager, teacher, expert, classmate, or the person in the next cubicle. Don't automatically assume you need to ask the most knowledgeable person you're aware of—you might be surprised what the average person in your new group knows.

If you aren't sure whom to ask, recognize that sometimes the most *immediately* helpful person isn't necessarily the one who *has* the answer, but may be the person *who can point you to those who have the answer*. Often changing your question from "Do you know . . . " to "Who do you know that . . ." can dramatically expand the number of people to whom you might first start your search.

Who Seems Friendly and Approachable?

Of all the people who might help you, who do you feel most comfortable approaching? You might factor a number of things into your thinking, and gravitate toward those who:

- You've successfully approached before.
- Have given you permission to ask questions.
- Seem to have a friendly, helpful personality.
- Seem the right kind of person to be asked this particular question.

Once again, remember we have a natural tendency to underestimate the approachability of others, especially busy, high-status people. And note that even though some people might seem perpetually grumpy and irritable, it doesn't automatically mean that they aren't open to answering questions, especially from new people.

Can I Interrupt Right Now?

You might also choose based on whether you feel it's okay to interrupt whatever the person is currently doing to ask your question. Sometimes it's clear when a person shouldn't or doesn't want to be disturbed, but often it's hard to tell.

Don't automatically assume that just because someone is busy, you're not allowed to approach the individual with a question. Realize that at work, and in many public activities, most of us are busy doing something *almost all of the time*. Just put yourself in the person's shoes and ask yourself if *you'd* be willing to be interrupted if you were doing what the person is doing. If so, go for it.

The social risk will also feel (and be) less if you approach, wait until you get the person's attention, and ask *if* you can ask a question:

"Is this a good time to ask a question?"

"Do you mind if I ask a question right now?"

"Got a minute to answer a question of mine, or should I come back later?"

This strategy gives the other person the choice to answer the question now or suggest a later time. Giving the person a sense of how long answering the question might take can also help them decide if and when to answer. For example, "I'm wondering if you can show me the proper format for this report. I think with five minutes of explanation I should be good to go." Either way, you can lessen the potential cost of the imposition by giving the other person some control over the size and scope of the interruption.

Three Words that Make Asking Any Question Easier

When it comes to asking strangers questions, recognize that you have a secret weapon that will make others:

- More willing to interrupt what they are doing and help you.
- Less inclined to think badly of you for asking a "dumb" question.
- Forgive your initial mistakes and blunders.

It's called being new.

Here's a little test: Pretend that you're working, and an unfamiliar person comes up to you and says the following: "Hi, my name is Sarah. Do you know where we keep the office supplies?" How would you react?

Now imagine she says: "Hi, my name is Sarah. I'm new here; this is my first day in the office. Do you know where we keep the office supplies?"

See the difference? By prefacing your question with some variant of the phrase "I'm new here," you do several things. You often reduce the social risk of interrupting someone by helping the person view your intrusion as the action of a newcomer. Most people not only expect newcomers to ask questions, but they also recognize that new people won't automatically know any special norms the group might have about when and where it's appropriate to ask questions. Instead of seeing you as an annoying interrupter, the person will just see you as new.

Using the "I'm new here" strategy also ensures that the person will also evaluate your question *in the context of your newness*. What may seem like a dumb question from someone who's been there a while is often seen as perfectly reasonable from a newcomer. It also helps ensure the *answer* is appropriate to your newcomer status. People often provide a more comprehensive, detailed response if they know you are completely new to a situation.

Finally, many groups and organizations have social norms encouraging members to be welcoming and supportive of newcomers. Declaring your newness right away may trigger that helping response. Depending on the situation, there are many ways to phrase this, including:

"This is my first time here. . . . "
"I've just joined. . . ."
"I've never done this before. . . . "

This strategy works best with complete strangers; once people know you are new, repeatedly reminding them of it will seem strange.

THE ART OF ASKING QUESTIONS

There are so many types of questions and so many question-asking situations that it's hard to give specific advice. Some things to keep in mind are:

- *Keep it short*. The longer you take to ask the question, the harder it is for the other person to make sense of it.

- *Briefly explain why you're asking.* If saying you're new isn't enough, provide a few sentences explaining why you're asking this particular question and what you'll do with the answer.
- *Demonstrate that you've done your homework.* If you're worried that the question is something that you should have figured out on your own, a sentence or two describing what you've already done to find or generate the answer—showing what you already know—may help reduce the social risk.
- *Avoid multi-part questions.* If you ask several questions at once, most people won't be able to remember your first one.
- *Listen to the answer.* Sometimes we're so busy thinking about the *next* question we want to ask we don't listen to the answer to our *current* question.
- *Ask follow-up questions, but only if needed.* Often the first question leads to additional questions.
- *Don't overstay your welcome.* If you sense you are taking up more time than the person wants to give you, ask if it's okay to come back later.
- *Say thank you.* It's obvious, but don't forget to thank the person for the information. If someone really went out of his or her way to help you, an email (sometimes cc'ed to the person's boss, teacher, or coach) can go a long way toward not only expressing your gratitude but also priming the person to help you in the future.
- *Close the loop.* If appropriate, let the person know later how the information ultimately helped you accomplish something. If people see their actions had an impact, they often are more likely to help you in the future.

Find a Buddy

When it comes to asking questions, one of the best things you can do when you're new is to find a buddy who is simultaneously:

- Helpful (or knows someone who will be)
- Approachable (with little social risk)
- Interruptible (within reason)
- Forgiving (of your "dumb" questions)

This person may be your boss, mentor, or teacher, but often a good buddy is someone located nearby in a role of equal status; it's also someone who isn't new but hasn't been around forever. That way he may still remember what it's like to a newcomer, and will empathize with the awkwardness of asking "dumb" questions. He may even retain some of his "newcomer's mindset" and, therefore, can put answers in a form that makes sense to someone new.

How to Reflect, Practice, and Get Better at Asking Questions

Surprise, surprise: the best way to get more comfortable asking questions is through reflection and mindful, deliberate practice. The best radio and TV journalists weren't born with the ability to confidently and comfortably ask questions of high-status, busy people. They honed their skill through hundreds of interviews and thousands of questions, as well as by reviewing and reflecting on their question-asking performance. You can, too. Here are three steps that move you in that direction:

1. Examine the Reasons for Your Reluctance
Think back to past newcomer situations in which you were reluctant to approach someone and ask a question. What caused you to hesitate? Were you worried more about interrupting and bothering the person with your question? Were you worried more what the person might think of you for asking it? Were you worried more about your ego and about accepting the fact you had to ask for help?

Then, look for patterns to your reluctance. For example,

Are you more reluctant to ask questions of certain *types* of people—for example, bosses, experts, teachers, or coaches? Men or women? Different cultural backgrounds?

Does it make a difference whether they are total strangers or recent acquaintances? If they are total strangers, are you more anxious about introducing yourself or asking your question?

How much does the presence of other people affect your reluctance? Are you more worried about what the person you are asking might think, or of what others hearing you ask the question might think?

How much do expectations of expertise play into your reluctance? Are you more reluctant to ask questions when others think you're a total beginner, or when others think you're already an expert?

Armed with these insights, you'll be better equipped to target your practice to the kinds of situations and questions that cause your anxiety and reluctance.

2. Observe Yourself Asking Questions

One of the main reasons you don't get more comfortable asking questions is that you haven't mindfully observed and reflected on what happened when you have asked questions. Had you done this, you would have seen that the social risk involved in approaching and asking someone a question is usually much lower than your hardwired, prehistoric brain and your early experiences have taught you to think they were.

Make a personal commitment to mindfully observe the questions you ask over the next few days and weeks. Note which ones you ask without hesitation or thought, and which ones cause you reluctance and anxiety. Does the pattern give you further clues to why you have an underlying anxiety to ask certain people or ask certain types of questions?

Then, each time you ask a question, try to step outside yourself and observe the entire process and consider the outcome. Ask yourself the following questions:

- How did the other person respond to your initial interruption and request to ask a question? Did the person seem annoyed or open to the intrusion? What signals did the person send that led you to that determination?
- How well did you ask your question? As you listened to yourself making your request, did it seem clear? Succinct? Confident? Did you provide enough context to explain why you were asking the question?
- What was the quality of the response? Did it answer your question? If it didn't, was it the result of a poorly asked question or the person's inability to answer it?
- What was the emotional energy in the response? Did the person answer your question with enthusiasm, reluctance, annoyance, or frustration? Was the person flattered that you came to ask a question?
- Based on the person's response, what do you think *his or her* underlying judgment was? Did the person seem to think you were an idiot for asking?
- Was the person's response any different from what yours would have been if the roles were reversed and you were being asked the question?
- Was your initial reluctance justified? Did your fears come true, or were you pleasantly surprised by the exchange?
- Did you end the conversation in a way that will make it easier to ask the person questions in the future?
- In hindsight, what could you have done differently to ask the question better? What about the experience can you remember and remind yourself about that would make it less awkward and make you less anxious the next time you ask a question?

The more you mindfully observe and reflect on your question-asking, the easier it will be to identify strategies to get better and more confident at it. Keeping a diary of these reflections may also be helpful, as not only does it provide "hard data" that you can analyze later for patterns, but also the act of writing them down can generate higher quality reflection.

3. Find Opportunities to Practice

Armed with reflective observation, you're ready to find and take advantage of opportunities to practice asking questions, especially the kinds that trigger your reluctance. As you go about your day, you'll find countless opportunities to ask questions. Obviously, you can practice asking questions in whatever new situation you're facing and care about, but sometimes the best places to practice asking questions are those situations where the social cost isn't high—or at least the long-term impact on your life is minimal. Let your curiosity be your guide, and try to ask questions when you have some real interest in knowing the answer.

Here are some possibilities:

- Ask salespeople, waiters, and clerks questions about products and services as you shop, order food, and make purchases.
- At work, ask questions of office administrators, cafeteria workers, and janitors.
- Ask questions of people you meet on trains, planes, organized trips, concerts, or sporting events.
- Stop and ask for directions (even if you have a GPS).

As you go about your day, look for opportunities to ask questions. Look especially for situations in which you know you've felt reluctance in the past, and then commit to approach and ask your questions anyway, mindfully reflecting on the experience as you move through it. If it helps, make a personal commitment to ask one question in each place you visit or event you attend. If you're worried about how well you will ask your question, rehearse the question in your mind before approaching the other person.

If your reluctance is primarily caused by asking high-status people your questions, then look for those kinds of opportunities. For example, at work look for opportunities to ask your boss and higher-ups some questions. Outside of work, ask questions of doctors, ministers, police officers, or politicians—anyone you've been reluctant to ask in the past (or expect you would be reluctant to ask in the future).

If your reluctance is mostly caused by the possibility of bothering busy people, then look for opportunities to practice interrupting people with a polite request for help, and reflect on their response. Obviously, you don't want to interrupt critical work or ask meaningless questions, but explore the limits of interrupting people doing their normal activities, even if they appear busy.

Experiment with leading statements like "I'm new here" or "This is my first time" as appropriate, and see how people respond to the admission that you're a newcomer. Try asking questions without that lead-in and compare the different responses, if any.

Think of the world as your personal "driving range," with lots of opportunities to drive home a mindfully asked question. Or, if it helps, pretend you're a journalist gathering research on a particular topic; sometimes taking on a journalist's mindset can provide the internal justification for asking your questions.

FIVE STEPS TO SUCCESSFULLY ASKING QUESTIONS

When we're new, asking questions is often the only way we can quickly get up to speed and be a successful newcomer. To overcome your reluctance, before asking a question:

1. Build a relationship with people you might have to ask questions of before ever having to ask a question.

2. Consider what you want and why you want it.

3. Determine whom to ask and if the time is right. Ask yourself: Who might be helpful? Who seems friendly and approachable? Can I interrupt right now?

4. Cultivate the art of asking questions; remember to keep it short, explain why you're asking, demonstrate you've done your homework, avoid multi-part questions, ask follow-up questions (but only if needed), say thank you, and don't overstay your welcome. Also, remember to close the loop, if needed, by letting the person you asked know the outcome.

5. Last but not least, find a buddy who can guide you when you're new.

You will become more comfortable and confident if you just get out there, ask lots of questions, and mindfully reflect on your experiences. Don't expect you'll turn into a confident question-asker overnight. It takes time to rewire your brain and unlearn old habits and assumptions, but you'll get there!

EIGHT

STARTING NEW RELATIONSHIPS

It doesn't matter if we're new to a job, school, church, health club, or neighborhood. Our success and happiness are often determined by our ability to start new relationships and integrate ourselves into new groups. In this chapter we will explore why we are reluctant to start and develop new relationships, and learn how we can improve our ability to move beyond the initial introduction and build positive, productive relationships with all sorts of people.

Through new relationships we:

- Get the information, help, and advice we need to get up to speed quickly
- Build the connections and collaborations we need to perform our new role and get work done
- Receive the social support we need to help us take risks, try new things, and persist through early stumbles
- Satisfy our primal need to belong and feel accepted

Sometimes new situations are temporary, and the relationships we create last only a few minutes. Other times we join new groups with the hope that the relationships we form will last a long time and bring us energy, success, and deep satisfaction for years. If we're new leaders, almost everything we achieve is accomplished through others. We succeed or fail based on how quickly and how well we can develop productive relationships with people across (and even outside) the organization.

We are fundamentally social animals, and researchers have repeatedly shown that relationships matter. Here is how one newcomer I interviewed described the power of relationships to transform how he viewed his new job:

> "I worked in support, which was a big group and we had to communicate back and forth. All of the new hires developed a tight bond with each other, and we began to go out for happy hours, or go to concerts on the weekends. We became really close. I didn't expect that. I couldn't wait to go to work and be with my best friends. It was work but it didn't feel like work. More like college."

Relationship expert Ellen Berscheid argues that "there is nothing people consider more meaningful and essential to their mental and physical well-being than their close relationships with other people"[1] Relationships are particularly important during major life changes such as new jobs, new schools, marriage, parenthood, and retirement—precisely all the events that put us into new situations. When we're new we use relationships to help us cope with the uncertainty and stress that come with the unfamiliar. If we want to fit in and find acceptance in new groups, our success is almost entirely determined by how well we start and develop new relationships.

Given all the benefits of relationships, why are we sometimes reluctant to take the first step and proactively start new relationships? Why do we:

- Wait for other people to make the first move (which often never comes)?
- Feel less connected and integrated over time than we had hoped to be?

Many newcomers I've interviewed are more apprehensive about developing new relationships than about performing their new role. One new MBA student was anxious about "fitting in" to a business school environment:

> "I never felt like I would fit in with business-type people. I have some social anxiety and worried if I would fit in and get along, see eye to eye. I was less worried about the academics than I was about making friends. I wasn't afraid of the type of work or the workload . . . but I worried about the social aspects."

Some people I've interviewed are comfortable making friends socially, but they are concerned about developing relationships at work:

> "I like to think that socially I have little problem meeting people, but in professional situations I am more closely guarded. I consider how I might be perceived from a work and professional standpoint, and how knowledgeable I appear. If I go up and ask what someone does I never know how I'll be received."

Others have the opposite view:

> "If I am in a position of authority and have to be outgoing and welcoming and sociable, I'll do it. But otherwise I'll often stand in the background. . . . I'm fine with people I have something in common with, but I'm not the kind of person who likes to walk into a party of people I don't know."

If you are like any of these folks, with a little understanding and a few strategies, you can become more comfortable and confident starting the kinds of relationships you want and need to be successful and happy.

WHY WE ARE RELUCTANT TO DEVELOP NEW RELATIONSHIPS

Not surprisingly, the same things that make us reluctant to introduce ourselves and ask questions also make us uncomfortable starting new relationships. One of the reasons humans came to dominate the planet is that we discovered the power of living in groups. Over time, being part of a group became so important to survival that being excluded or rejected by one's group was practically a death sentence.

As a result, we came to fear social rejection. From the brain's perspective, social rejection "hurts" in much the same way that physical pain does. Researchers have even shown that taking the pain reliever acetaminophen actually helps alleviate the sadness that comes with social rejection.[2]

Fear of Social Rejection

Often we're sensitive to (and fear) two types of social rejection. One is getting rejected and excluded because other people don't like us. The other is getting rejected because we're imposing ourselves on people who don't want another relationship. Unless we're part of a newly formed group where no one knows each other (such as a group of incoming college freshmen), we are usually joining a group with an existing set of relationships.

In those situations, we may worry that the others are happy with the quantity and quality of their current relationships, and don't need or desire one more. As one newcomer put it:

"The number of people you meet and get to know depends somewhat on how well people on the team you join already know each other. The more they know each other beforehand the harder it can be, especially if they already have people to eat dinner and chill out with, and aren't looking for another [relationship]."

In order to avoid social rejection, we've evolved a very sophisticated sociometer in our brains, which is highly sensitive to signs that we might be or are being excluded or ostracized.[3] When we're new, that sociometer is often in overdrive as we try to figure out how well we're being accepted by our new group members.

For much of human history this internal sociometer was a very useful thing. Often we were only a few rejections away from becoming an outcast. But these days we live in a world where being rejected is rarely life-threatening unless exclusion and dislike are accompanied by physical violence and deprivation, which is rare in most situations. Most of the time there is another group we can join, another job we can take, or another person we can befriend.

The problem is that our brains aren't hardwired to separate serious from less serious rejections.[4] It's still easy for us to perceive every potential rejection as a threat to our existence. As a result, we:

- Worry about being accepted by people we'll probably never meet again
- Fear being disliked by people who ultimately have little influence over (or interest in) our lives
- Stress over every new relationship, even though we know we usually have lots of alternatives

We don't even like rejection from people we hate. Researchers Karen Gonsalkorale and Kipling Williams conducted a clever study using a ball-tossing video game in which the subjects believed that they were playing "virtual catch" with several other people.[5] The game was manipulated so that the subjects found themselves excluded from the game (i.e., nobody passed them the ball anymore). The result was that people felt bad when they were excluded, even if they thought they were playing catch with members of the Ku Klux Klan, a despised white supremacy group. Other researchers have used the same video game and found that people automatically react negatively to being excluded, even if they know they are just playing "virtual catch" with a computer.[6]

It gets worse. Researchers have also shown that if we enter into new relationships fearing or expecting rejection, we often perceive rejection even when it's not there. In one study, researchers told participants that they would be having two short get-acquainted sessions with a stranger. A few minutes after the first session, the researchers informed one participant that the other person didn't want to continue with the experiment. Those participants who expressed a higher sensitivity to rejection interpreted the other person's refusal to continue as a personal rejection, and felt bad afterwards. Those participants who expressed a lower sensitivity to rejection didn't take it personally, and experienced no change in mood.[7] The takeaway is that if we automatically fear social rejection we're not only more reluctant to approach someone and start a relationship, we're more likely to interpret any ambiguous or tentative reaction by the other person as rejection, even if it really isn't.

It's not just our evolutionary history that makes us fear social rejection. Many of us also learn to fear it from a young age. Sometimes it comes from direct personal experience of being excluded or ignored by siblings or playmates. Other times it comes from seeing the impact that rejection and exclusion has on other kids. Countless movies and TV shows also set up completely unrealistic expectations about new relationships, and teach us that social rejection is mostly the domain of dweebs, misfits, and losers. No wonder we grow up with a reinforced fear of social rejection.

Uncertainty about the "Rules of the Game"

Some of our anxiety comes from unclear social norms concerning how to start and maintain relationships. For example, when is it appropriate to start a conversation with the stranger sitting next to you at a concert? How soon after meeting a co-worker can you invite the person to lunch? At what point is it okay to ask another person for a favor?

Not only are these norms uncertain and variable, but we discover them mostly by trial and error. Also, strategies that work well when we're children are often problematic as adults. For example, in preschool we often can start a new relationship by just walking up to another kid and saying "Will you be my friend?" Try that with an adult; you may not be hit with a restraining order, but you'll almost certainly get the cold shoulder.

Complicating matters is the fact that there are often major differences in norms across cultures for starting and maintaining relationships. In some parts of the world, a relationship implies a set of very specific expectations and obligations around things like gift-giving, inviting, visiting, hosting, and favor-returning. In other parts of the world, relationships are more casual. While etiquette books can offer lots of good advice, the uncertainty created by our increasingly globalized world only makes us more reluctant to approach others to try to start new relationships.

Social Networking's Impact on Modern Relationships

These days, we also face a more insidious problem when it comes to starting relationships. Compared to our ancestors, we have so many more ways to satisfy our need for relationships. Before there were books, reality TV shows, and binge watching on Netflix, the only relationships we had were face-to-face ones with real people. Now we can easily stay in contact with old friends and acquaintances, reducing our need to create new ones. We can build up a large (but relatively anonymous and often superficial) set of virtual relationships on social media, and convince ourselves that online friends are just as good as face-to-face ones.

Furthermore, many of us end up gravitating to the vicarious relationships we develop with people in books and TV shows. We quickly discover that it's impossible for a book or TV character to reject us. These vicarious "friends" are also available 24/7, and they usually live far more interesting lives than we do.

Scientists call these *parasocial relationships*, and they have shown that the more we consume them, the more we start to see the characters as real, and the more we mourn their departure from our lives when the books and TV series end.[8] Researcher Mark Leary hypothesizes that evolution may play an unwitting part in our use and sometimes preference for these kinds of relationships. Because stories, books, and TV shows are only a recent addition to human existence, our brains may process and react to fake relationships in much the same way that we do to real ones.[9]

These kinds of parasocial relationships don't necessarily make us more reluctant to start new face-to-face relationships, but they do give us an easy, convenient substitute that may keep us from starting and developing the relationships we really need and value. Unfortunately, outside of work and family relationships, many people spend far more hours per day with their fake TV and book "friends" than with their real ones.

STRATEGIES FOR DEVELOPING NEW RELATIONSHIPS

When we're new we often face a paradox in developing relationships. We need to develop relationships in order to feel comfortable in new situations, but we need to feel comfortable in order to start new relationships. The challenge is finding a way to break that cycle, overcome our natural fear of social rejection, and find the courage to move past initial introductions and try to create the relationships we want.

When you're new, one of the easiest and most effective ways to become more comfortable and confident in starting relationships is to have a strategy and an action plan. This doesn't mean that you want to turn relationship development and making friends into some kind of cold, calculating influence scheme. It does mean that you can dramatically reduce the stress and awkwardness in new situations by taking some time to think about:

- What you need and want out of new relationships
- What kinds of relationships you want to pursue
- Which are must-have versus nice-to-have relationships
- How you might approach and interact with new people in ways that potentially start and strengthen relationships
- What upcoming opportunities (identified or created) exist to start relationships

Sometimes you'll have days and weeks to think about where, what, and with whom you might try to build new relationships. Other times you'll do it on the fly in a few seconds as you walk into organizing meetings, parties, or networking events. The key is to be purposeful in your actions, realistic in your expectations, and mindful of your approach (and what transpires).

Be Purposeful in Your Actions

When you enter a new situation, the first question to ask yourself is what you hope to achieve and receive from the relationships you form.

Determine What You Want from the Relationship

Depending on the situation, you could have a variety of needs and desires, such as:

- Information, advice, and help
- Collaboration to achieve common goals

- Understanding , caring, and emotional support
- Companionship and friendship

What we want in new situations often varies. In a new job or school, we probably want our emerging relationships to satisfy all these needs and last a long time. But at a hardware store, all we want from our five-minute, temporary relationship with the sales clerk is information, help, and advice. And on a long plane flight, all we might want from our seatmates is perhaps companionship to pass the time.

Determine with Whom to Have a Relationship

Once you clarify what you want from a new relationship, you can start identifying candidates who might meet those needs. Depending on the situation there are a variety of things you might consider:

- Roles and responsibilities (yours and theirs)
- Proximity and availability
- Expertise and helpfulness
- Approachability and friendliness
- Similarity (of roles, interests, backgrounds, etc.)

Obviously, there are some people with whom you *must* develop new relationships, such as your new boss, teacher, or coach. But often there are many people who could equally satisfy a particular need or set of needs. The more potential relationships you can identify, the more backup options you have if you try to develop a relationship and it just doesn't materialize.

Also, recognize that different people will likely satisfy different needs. At your new job you might seek to collaborate with new teammates to get your work done. But you also might seek help and assistance from a mentor or office administrator, understanding and emotional support from one of your more friendly office neighbors, and companionship from some of the other newcomers you met in orientation. If you're new to a health club, you might seek advice and help from a trainer, but want companionship from others taking the same aerobics class.

Why does this matter? Understanding what you want in a relationship and who might satisfy those needs sets you up to figure out what kinds of relationships you want to develop when you're new.

Determine What Kind of Relationship You Want to Develop

You have some choice and control over how strong a relationship you might want to develop. While it's often impossible to predict where any particular relationship will end up, it's important to recognize there are varying levels of interaction and intimacy.

Relationships between Co-Participating Strangers. You typically start these kinds of relationships when you interact with strangers in some sort of shared activity or experience but don't introduce yourselves. This includes situations such as:

- Sitting next to strangers at concerts, sporting events, lectures, and other performances
- Standing in line at the coffee shop or airport
- Store purchases or service interactions (e.g., retail, restaurants, hair salons, etc.)

It might not feel like much of a relationship, but it is. During this shared activity you will likely interact in ways defined by your respective roles (e.g., concert-goers, classmates, passengers, buyer and sellers, customer and service provider). But often you'll also engage in small talk and friendly banter. Frequently the conversation will initially revolve around what you're doing together, but it can eventually go anywhere. Through these interactions you may express opinions on what you're collectively experiencing, commiserate over problems and long delays, or simply chat about the weather.

Often these are temporary relationships with people we'll never see again. But sometimes we meet the same "strangers" over and over. Either way, we often gain quite a bit from these types of relationships, including help, advice, companionship, understanding, and even emotional support. Sometimes they might even be better than more extensive or deeper relationships. If you know you're making both a first and last impression on a stranger you'll likely never see again, you can just be yourself, enjoy the moment, and not worry too much about social costs and long-term consequences.

Relationships with Acquaintances. You typically start these kinds of relationships as soon as you've introduced yourselves, exchanged names, and made small talk. Most us have made hundreds or thousands of these relationships already, and will likely make many more in the future. Through acquaintances we can satisfy many of our relationship needs including help, companionship, and emotional support.

Much like co-participating strangers, some acquaintances you will never see again. Others you will continue to repeatedly run into for the rest of your life. Either way, the exchange of names and personal information sets up an expectation that the next time you see each other you will recognize, acknowledge, and remember something about them.[10]

Relationships with Colleagues, Classmates, and Co-members. You typically develop these kinds of relationships when you start working together as part of a group to accomplish something meaningful. This includes all sorts of new situations from work teams and project groups to volunteer organizations and church committees.

Often your interactions are defined by your respective roles in the group, and over time you come to know and rely upon each other to get things done. Through colleagues we not only get the collaboration, help, and advice we need to successfully perform our new role, but we also satisfy our needs for companionship and belonging. Once you stop working together, these kinds of collegial relationships often drift back to just being acquaintances.

Relationships with Teachers, Mentors, and Coaches. One of the best ways to ensure success in new situations is to establish and nurture relationships with people who can serve as teachers, mentors, and coaches. These people can:

- Help you make sense of your new experiences.
- Give you timely, expert information and advice.
- Provide emotional and/or organizational support as you try to accomplish your goals.
- Role-model successful behaviors.[11]

Relationships with Friends. You begin turning acquaintances and colleagues into friends once you start inviting each other to things that are outside normal group activities (e.g., invitations to lunch, movies, hikes, golf outings, etc.) or disclosing and trusting each other with more personal information about yourself.

Though it's a bit of an oversimplification, men tend to form friendships through common interests and activities, while women tend to form relationships through self-disclosure and sharing.[12] Though you can often obtain information, help, and advice from many kinds of relationships, it's only through friends that you often can get the companionship, understanding, caring, and emotional support you need to be truly happy.

What kind of relationships should you strive for in a new situation? It all depends on what you want. In most new situations you'll end up with a mixture of these relationships. When you're new, it's hard to predict how specific relationships will progress. Ultimately, what really matters is getting a mix of relationships that meet your wants and needs and that gives you the success, satisfaction, and happiness you desire.

HOW TO APPROACH STARTING NEW RELATIONSHIPS

After you've thought a bit about what you want from new relationships, who good prospects might be, and the kinds of relationships you want to develop, the next step is to decide how you will start new relationships. Since Chapter 5 explored the methods of introductions, here we focus on how you can move beyond the introduction and build new relationships with more comfort and confidence.

Researchers have found there are many strategies and approaches that can make a difference, including:

- Putting yourself in their shoes
- Focusing on giving others energy
- Staying positive and saying nice things about other people
- Using reciprocity to build relationships
- Giving priority to others' needs, without neglecting your own
- Imagining you are a detective, journalist, or party host
- Inviting others to "outside" activities

Put Yourself in the Other Person's Shoes

As with introductions and asking questions, many newcomers are also reluctant to approach and develop relationships with new people. Many worry the other person won't be interested in them, or will be annoyed by the approach and interruption, or will not want to start another relationship. But, as with introductions and asking questions, when the tables are turned and new people approach them with an honest, sincere desire to interact, it's a different story. In most cases, they are quite happy to stop what they're doing and have a friendly conversation; in fact, they realize that as established members, they have an obligation to welcome new people. Usually they appreciate it when newcomers take the initiative, as it saves them the social risk of making the first move.

More important, when newcomers approach, people seem to spend much less time worrying about being rejected by that person; also, they don't even think much about whether they should ultimately accept or reject the newcomer.

So, in new situations, take a moment to ask yourself how you'd respond if you were the old-timer and new people approached you. If you'd be okay with it, just go for it.

Focus on Giving Others Energy

The key to starting new relationships is to realize that success is less about impressing the other person with your intelligence, achievements, and winning personality. It's more about ensuring that the other person gains energy from interacting with you.[13]

What tends to bring people energy are the same things that people want from relationships:

- Being understood.
- Having their ideas and opinions validated.
- Being valued, respected, and accepted.
- Accomplishing something meaningful.
- Receiving help (when they want it).
- Having fun.

It's not surprising, then, that a focus on energy is effective in building relationships with extroverts. Extroverts get much of their energy from other people, so you'd expect that they would respond positively to people who give them energy. But this approach is probably an even more powerful and effective strategy with introverts.

Introverts generate much of their energy from within, and typically face a quandary when it comes to relationships. They desire relationships for all the good things that come from them—achievement, acceptance, companionship, and so on—but they find new social situations exhausting; they sense that, most of the time, they put more energy into interacting with others than they get back in return. If they remain quiet (or the extroverts dominate the conversation), it only makes it worse, as few people gain energy just by listening to other people talk. Imagine how introverts will feel about you if you can find a way to provide them energy in social situations?

One of the most powerful and simplest ways to help people gain energy is by demonstrating sincere interest in them. Showing interest tends to get people talking, and most people gain energy by talking a bit about themselves (and what they know). More important, by showing interest, you are providing understanding, appreciation, validation, respect, and acceptance, not to mention companionship.[14]

This is hardly a new idea. In 1936, Dale Carnegie published what is probably the most successful and bestselling self-help book of all time. *How to Win Friends and Influence People* is still on the bestseller lists almost eighty years later. One of his most powerful and enduring relationship-building suggestions is to show interest in other people by asking questions and listening intently to the answers.

Since Carnegie, other researchers have proved in countless studies that this really works.[15] In particular, they've shown that people:

- Like strangers who reveal a little bit (but not too much) about themselves.
- Disclose more information about themselves to strangers they initially like.
- Like strangers even more after they've had the opportunity to talk about themselves.

Therefore, to get strangers to like you right away (and leave with a positive first impression of you), your best strategy is to get them talking about themselves (or what they know), and find opportunities to say a little bit about yourself.

Stay Positive and Say Nice Things About Other People

In your conversations with new people, try to stay positive. Most people do not gain energy by hearing (or talking about) negative things. Furthermore, researchers have discovered that if, when talking with strangers, you say nice things about other people, strangers often walk away thinking you have those qualities, too.[16]

For example, if you happen to tell a stranger that your manager is generous and kind, that stranger is likely to remember you as also generous and kind. Conversely, if you rant about what a selfish jerk your manager is, you run the risk of strangers remembering you in much the same way.

Use Reciprocity to Develop Relationships

Whether they are superficial and temporary, or deep and long-lasting, all relationships are built on reciprocity. Other people help us meet our needs, and in turn we have an instinctive urge (and there is often a social expectation) to help them in return. Scientists call this *reciprocal altruism*, and we're both hardwired and taught from an early age to return favors and repay our debts. Many of the things we want in relationships—trust, reliability, integrity, and so on—have their basis in our fundamental need for reciprocity.

How does this play out in new relationships? When you help people gain energy through listening, appreciation, and companionship, they start to have a positive impression of you. Reciprocity predisposes them to help you gain energy in return. In turn, you form a positive impression of them, and are predisposed to find other ways (and opportunities) to help them gain energy. Round and round it goes, and the relationship develops and deepens.

This doesn't mean that we help each other gain energy in the same way in all situations. For example, at work you may help your new boss complete a report, and she may return the favor by publicly thanking you for your efforts. She gains energy from your help, and you gain energy from your boss's recognition. At school you might lend an attentive, sympathetic ear to your new dorm mate, and he may invite you along to a party. He gains understanding and support, and you gain a social opportunity.

Nor does reciprocity always happen at the same time or be perfectly equal. You might comfort an acquaintance after a tough breakup, and three months later, she shows up to help you move to a new apartment. Or, you may spend a weekend revising a marketing analysis for a co-worker and in the moment just get a smile and a sincere thank-you in return. What matters is that, over time, both parties feel reasonably good about what they give and get from the relationship.[17]

Give Priority to Other People's Needs, but Don't Neglect Your Own

Since people gain energy when their needs are met, you need to figure out what they want and help them get it. But you also want to make sure that interacting with them will ultimately bring you energy, too. Otherwise you may have little incentive to continue.

This is easier said than done, especially in new situations. For some of us, our tendency is to unconsciously dominate the conversation and talk too much about ourselves and what we know, perhaps because we:

- Want to make a good first impression and have come to believe (consciously or unconsciously) that talking a lot is the best approach.
- Feel we have a great deal to contribute to the conversation and others will benefit from our knowledge and expertise.
- Gain energy from talking and it's become a habit.

Regardless of the reason, the result is that we spend little time trying to identify or meet the other person's needs. And since few people gain much energy from listening to us talk all the time, blathering on is a great way to turn people off. Sadly, we're often the last ones to realize that we are dominating the conversation.

On the other hand, some of us end up talking too little about ourselves and what we know because we:

- Worry about saying something that will make us look bad.
- Prefer being private and reserved in what we disclose about ourselves.
- Don't like "fighting for air time" with highly talkative people.
- Tend to lose interest and disengage from long conversations.

As a result, we end up spending little time doing things that meet *our* needs and bring *us* energy. Some of this is caused by the other person, but some of it is the result of our reluctance to speak up, change the conversation, or strive to get what we want. Either way, we may walk away from the interaction with both less energy and less motivation to take the initiative and approach others in the future. Ultimately, the best, most productive, and satisfactory relationships are ones where everyone is attentive to both their own and the other person's needs.

Imagine You Are a Party Host, Detective, or Journalist

One way to overcome your reluctance to approach and start new relationships, and ensure that you interact in ways that bring others energy, is by adopting the mindset and actions of a party host, detective, or journalist.

For example, as you walk into a party, social, or networking event, pretend that you're one of the organizers and hosts and your job is to ensure that everyone is having a good time. One newcomer I interviewed described this approach and its benefits:

"I assume everyone else is as uncomfortable as I am, and it's my duty to make them more comfortable, which helps me forget that I'm uncomfortable. . . . Also by getting to know someone and making them feel more comfortable I create an ally, which in turn makes me more comfortable."

In his book *Just Listen*, clinical psychologist Mark Goulston encourages people to adopt a detective's mindset as a way of showing interest in others:

"How do you master the skill of being interested—and be sincere when you do it? The first key is to stop thinking of conversation as a tennis match. (He scored a point. Now I need to score a point.) Instead, think of it as a detective game, in which your goal is to learn as much about the other person as you can. Go into the conversation knowing that there is something very interesting about the person, and be determined to discover it."[18]

A third approach is to pretend you're a journalist whose job is to interview the people you want to meet. One newcomer I interviewed had a sister-in-law who happened to be a reporter. Her sister-in-law discovered that the job actually helped her overcome her anxiety around strangers, and she continued to adopt a journalist's strategy in other social situations. Here is how she described it:

"My sister-in-law was a reporter. . . . [S]he has severe social anxiety but you would never know it because she is very good at putting people at ease. Her tactic was to ask questions. . . . People like to talk about themselves. She has met many of my friends and they all think she is great, but they don't know how nervous she is. They like her without realizing they've mostly had a whole conversation about themselves."

These approaches may help reduce your anxiety by:

- Helping you act in ways that bring others energy, especially by showing interest in them.
- Keeping your mind off your own negative thoughts and fears.
- Providing you a built-in justification (even if only pretend) for approaching new people.
- Keeping you from talking too much.

Obviously, you don't want to take these personas too far and look silly, but give one a try and see if it helps. Researchers use the term *openers* to describe people who are good at getting other people to talk about themselves. Several studies have shown that openers tend to be liked, especially by strangers.[19]

Invite Them to "Outside" Activities

It's somewhat obvious, but at some point one of the best ways to strengthen a relationship is to invite someone to lunch, coffee, or some other activity that is separate from your normal interactions. Inviting (or accepting the invitation of others) to outside events or activities accomplishes the following:

- It sends a signal that you're interested in getting to know the person better, and perhaps pursue a friendship.
- It provides an opportunity to socialize in ways you often can't in your regular group interactions.
- It gives you a chance to ask "newcomer" questions without worrying about interrupting a busy person.

The key is to have the courage to either make or accept the invitation, even if the introvert in you wants to stay (or head straight) home.

BE REALISTIC IN YOUR EXPECTATIONS

Regardless of your ultimate strategy, recognize that when it comes to starting relationships, not every approach will lead to a meaningful interaction, not every interaction will lead to a relationship, and not every relationship will progress the way you hope or expect it will.

Since all relationships require "two to tango," you often have some choice but only partial control on how things progress. Sometimes there just isn't the right chemistry, or the other person simply doesn't have the time or energy to put into a new relationship. Sometimes the other person is also uncomfortable starting new relationships and doesn't have the courage to reciprocate. Depending on the situation, starting new relationships, even at work, is often a numbers game. As one newcomer said:

> "I learned that it was almost a volume thing. If you want to develop more relationships, you have to meet a lot of people. You need to join clubs, go to parties, and don't talk just with your friends but talk to everyone else, too."

Don't put too much pressure on yourself to start lots of relationships quickly. Meeting a large group of strangers can be overwhelming. Pick a modest goal of getting to know two or three people, and if you start more relationships than that, it's a pleasant surprise. Once you've established a few relationships, you'll feel more comfortable and less anxious developing more.

If you give it your best shot, and it doesn't develop as you want it to, don't automatically see it either as a failure or a rejection of you. Learn from the experience, and try a slightly different approach the next time. As one newcomer I interviewed said:

> "I've come to learn that you're far better off interacting with other people than not. Experience will prove that interacting . . . makes life

better. That mentality will lead you to try to do it more often. You'll come to the realization that you can only benefit from it. There is nothing to lose by doing. . . . It becomes easier after you've been turned down a few times."

Ultimately, the easiest way *not* to get the relationships you want is to never try to start and develop them in the first place.

HOW TO REFLECT, PRACTICE, AND GET BETTER AT STARTING RELATIONSHIPS

In order to become more comfortable and confident starting new relationships, you need to explore and uncover the reasons for your reluctance and anxiety, mindfully observe how you think and act as you start relationships with new people, identify the strategies and approaches that work for you, and find opportunities to practice and experiment.

Think back to past situations where you've been reluctant to move past the initial interaction and start a new relationship. What caused you to hesitate or avoid taking the initiative? Was it:

- Fear of not being liked?
- Fear of imposing yourself upon people who already had an established set of relationships?
- Worry that you might violate prevailing social norms around starting relationships?
- A habit of waiting for the other person to make the first move?
- Easy alternatives to starting a new relationship (e.g., your existing relationships, vicarious relationships in books and TV shows, etc.)?

Next, look for patterns associated with your anxiety and reluctance. For example:

- Does your reluctance vary by type of relationship? Are you more anxious striking up conversations with co-participating strangers? Making and maintaining acquaintances? Building relationships with new colleagues? Taking the initiative to turn acquaintances and colleagues into friends?
- Are there certain kinds of new group situations in which you find it more difficult to start relationships? New jobs? New schools? New clubs or volunteer groups? New neighborhoods? Parties and social events?
- Do you find it harder to develop relationships with certain types of people? Bosses and those with higher status? People of different gender, race, age, or socioeconomic backgrounds?
- Does the number of people in the new group make a difference? Do you prefer the intimacy of one-on-one relationships and/or small groups or the relative anonymity of large groups?

By reflecting on the types of new situations and people that cause you the most anxiety and reluctance, you can focus your attention and practice on the right things.

BE MINDFUL OF YOUR APPROACH (AND WHAT TRANSPIRES)

Much of your anxiety and reluctance to start new relationships comes from assumptions, expectations, and habits that you've developed over a lifetime. By mindfully observing your thoughts and actions as you develop new connections, you can uncover these assumptions and see if they are truly justified and beneficial.

Over the next few weeks it is likely that you will have the opportunity to interact with and start relationships with relative strangers. Some may be associated with a new group you're joining, while others may be spontaneous interactions with random people. Just before you approach them, ask yourself:

- Why do I want to meet them?
- What need will I satisfy by starting a relationship with them? Collaboration? Information? Understanding and support? Companionship?
- What kind of relationship do I think I could have with them? Co-participating stranger? Acquaintance? Colleague? Potential friend?

As you contemplate approaching specific people, ask yourself:

1. What do they likely want or need from our interaction? How can I help them gain energy?
2. Am I feeling any reluctance to approach them? If so, what do I fear? Rejection? Dislike? Annoyance? Violating social norms?
3. Based on my past experience, what is the real probability that my fears of rejection will come true? What would happen if they did? How bad would that be?
4. Would it help to approach them pretending I'm a host, detective, or journalist?

Then as you start to interact and develop a relationship, observe what you both say and do and ask yourself the following:

1. How did they respond to my approach and opening lines?
2. Was I able to have and show sincere interest in what they were talking about? Did I ask questions to keep the conversation going? Did I talk too much or too little? Did I stay positive?
3. Overall, did they seem to gain energy from interacting with me? Did I gain energy from interacting with them?
4. What does this say about my underlying assumptions, expectations, and habits? What can I adjust or do differently the next time to be more comfortable and confident starting relationships with relative strangers?

If you initially feared social rejection, ask yourself: *Were my fears justified? Did they do or say anything to suggest they disliked me or were annoyed by my interruption?*

For those relationships that continue beyond the first few interactions:

1. Have I taken the initiative to strengthen the relationship? Invited them to an event or activity outside of our normal interactions? Accepted their invitations? How have they responded?
2. Am I trying too hard to develop this relationship? Not hard enough?
3. What are both of us gaining from the relationship? Does it seem mutually beneficial? Worth continuing?
4. What other relationships do I still need to start to achieve the success and happiness I want from this new situation?

If it helps, periodically write down some of your thoughts, fears, observations, and conclusions. Look for patterns and clues and use the information to adjust your strategies and approach to starting relationships.

FIND OPPORTUNITIES TO PRACTICE STARTING RELATIONSHIPS WITH STRANGERS

As you go about your daily activities, look for opportunities to practice interacting with people in ways that help start and develop relationships. This could include:

- Approaching and starting conversations with strangers while commuting, standing in line, waiting, or attending social events. Experiment with introducing (or not introducing) yourself during the conversation.
- Interacting more frequently and extensively with acquaintances (e.g., co-workers, classmates, neighbors, service providers, etc.).

- Finding opportunities to socialize with colleagues and group members outside of your normal interactions.

Obviously it's unethical and wrong to develop fake relationships (especially friendships) with people just to practice your relationship skills. But you can probably identify people you'd like to meet or get to know better, and in that case you are not simply practicing.

EVALUATE HOW WELL YOU FIT IN WITH YOUR NEW GROUP

One way to see "fitting in" with a group is to view it as the collective result of starting and building individual relationships with those in the group. Some of this will naturally happen as you collaborate with others to achieve group goals. Other times, you'll build these relationships through small talk, water cooler conversations, and outside activities.

In addition to helping others gain energy, there are other things that lead to positive relationships, including integrity, reliability, trustworthiness, humility, and credibility. You'll also want to ensure you show loyalty to the group and put the group's interests ahead of your own (when appropriate). While these factors impact the start of relationships, they are really critical to strengthening and maintaining relationships.

Finally, recognize that people talk with each other, so the positive relationships you start to build with one person can help you build relationships with other people. If others in your group have received advance information that you're a friendly, engaging, helpful person, it'll be easier to approach and build relationships with them as well.

FIVE STEPS TO SUCCESSFULLY STARTING NEW RELATIONSHIPS

When we're new, much of our success and happiness is determined by our ability to start and develop new relationships. But our fear of rejection makes us reluctant to approach and interact with relative strangers in ways that create positive, productive relationships. You can become more comfortable and confident starting new relationships if you:

1. Realize that both the risk and downside of social rejection is usually much less than your Stone Age brain and early childhood experiences lead you to believe.
2. Approach new situations with a clear idea of the mix and type of relationships that may get you what you want and need.
3. Start positive, productive relationships by focusing on others' needs, showing interest, staying positive, and interacting in ways that help others gain energy.
4. Take the time to reflect and uncover your underlying assumptions, expectations, and habits around starting relationships.
5. Find opportunities to practice starting, maintaining, and developing new relationships.

NINE

PERFORMING IN NEW SITUATIONS

In this chapter we will examine how we function in new situations, and learn how to improve our ability to:

- Do new things in front of people we don't know.
- Feel and be more comfortable and confident performing when we're new.
- Overcome performance anxiety.

It doesn't matter whether you're starting a new job, learning a new hobby, or trying out a new sport; almost everything you want to achieve in life requires you to not only put yourself into new situations but also *perform new things in front of unfamiliar people*. If you join your first sales organization, you have to become comfortable making cold calls and product presentations to strangers. If you want to learn how to ski, you have to figure out how to turn, stop, and get down the mountain in full view of other skiers. If you join a new health club, you often have to master new exercise equipment and aerobics routines alongside other members.

In interviewing newcomers, I've found that most people can point to something that they've been anxious or reluctant to perform in front of others when they're new. This includes things like leading an initial meeting as a new manager, playing a first round of golf, joining a master swim club, or taking a beginning painting class. In all of these situations, there is something specific that we:

- Need to perform to be successful.
- Learn mostly by doing.
- Start as a relative beginner.
- Perform in front of more experienced people.

For example, one newcomer found himself at his first bluegrass music jam, and discovered he was anxious about playing his instrument in front of others:

"I was both excited and nervous about having to play in front of others. . . . There was definitely anxiety there playing in a group. . . . It was nerve-wracking as I could tell I was not in sync with the group or it didn't feel quite right. I felt like I was absorbing lots of information but wasn't really able to contribute to the group yet."

Another newcomer felt pressure to perform well in a new yoga class, even though impressing others wasn't her main goal:

"Sometimes I feel like you need to show off your skills even when you might not want to . . . you go there. It isn't a place of comfort. You try to show off . . . even when that's not why you are there. It ends up becoming more a social challenge than a place of learning and exercise. When you're new that feeling is magnified, and you wonder if you have failed and why you should go back."

Performance anxiety isn't something that only shy and introverted people experience. One of the most extroverted newcomers I have ever interviewed was completely comfortable walking into a room full of strangers and walking out with a dozen new acquaintances. As she put it, "I warm up very quickly in groups. If I go to a party I quickly get out on my own and talk to everyone there. People will forget who I was attached to." But taking her first Crossfit exercise class was another story:

> "I was really intimidated and when I went there for the first time it was really emotional. I had to do a 7-minute routine in front of everyone watching me and I wasn't sure I could do that. . . . Now it's fun but then it was intimidating. . . . I thought I'd be far behind and it would be humiliating."

A little bit of anxiety (and the adrenaline it releases) can help you stay focused and alert, and can actually improve performance. But too much anxiety can cause you to:

- Perform more poorly and learn and improve more slowly than you normally would.
- Enjoy the experience less than you otherwise might.
- Procrastinate and find excuses not to do something.
- Give up too quickly.
- Or never even attempt it in the first place.

However, with a little bit of understanding and a few simple strategies and mindset shifts, you can become more comfortable and confident performing new things in front of unfamiliar people.

THE CAUSES OF PERFORMANCE ANXIETY

While there are many factors, performance anxiety often comes from the same inherited and learned fears we have in introducing ourselves, asking questions, and starting relationships. We're hardwired and thus predisposed to fear failure, rejection, and loss of social status. These anxieties are especially strong when we're performing new things in front of unfamiliar people and our social status is still unclear. We also learn at an early age to embrace a performance-oriented, "being good" mindset that causes us to worry excessively about making mistakes and looking bad in front of new people.

As we've seen, humans have a natural, genetic *fear of failure and social rejection*. Group life wasn't all warm and fuzzy; we competed for food, shelter, and mates. Often this competition turned violent, but all that fighting, injury, and death hurt the group's ability to survive, so we evolved *status hierarchies* as a way to create a more stable and effective group. Members still competed and sometimes fought, but only to establish and maintain the "pecking order" of social status from strongest to weakest. As a result, we evolved to care about and be sensitive to our social standing in groups. In fact, evolutionary psychologists believe that emotions like shame and embarrassment emerged as a way for our brain to keep us from performing (and especially repeating) things that might cause us to lose social status.[1]

It's not surprising, then, that we've evolved to be even more anxious performing *when we are new to a group*. With people we've known for a long time, our reputation is pretty well established, and it's unlikely that our next performance will have much impact on our long-term social status. But with new groups our social status is still unresolved, and it's easy to assume our early performances will have a big impact on where we end up in the group's status hierarchy.

Our brains are still hardwired that way, even though today:

- Many of our public performances take place in front of people we'll either never see again or who have little impact on our well-being.
- Having low social status in a new group is rarely dangerous or fatal.

- If we're not satisfied with our social status in one group, we can often move on and join another.

Though our genes may predispose us to be anxious performers, we also *learn* to worry about doing well when we're new to a group. Our anxiety comes from the *assumptions* and *mindsets* we acquire over time and bring to new performances. Educational researcher Carol Dweck and others have found that many of us learn at an early age to approach new experiences with the subconscious belief that we're born with a relatively fixed amount of skill and ability to do certain things.[2]

With this "talent is mostly fixed" mindset, we assume that when we try something new, we start to uncover our natural talent in that area. If we quickly master the role, task, or skill, we conclude we have a natural talent for it. If we struggle, make lots of mistakes, and see little initial progress, we decide that we're "just not that good at that sort of thing." As a result, success in life is all about discovering and taking advantage of the natural talents we're born with.

Sounds like a nice strategy, but here's the problem with a "talent is mostly fixed" mindset. Suppose we enter a new situation and conclude that a particular skill or ability is important for success and valued by the group. In that case, our initial performance becomes the "Big Reveal" of our natural talent. If we do well, we impress and gain the acceptance of our new group members. If we do poorly, we make a bad first impression and suggest to others (and ourselves) that we just don't have what it takes to be a productive, valued member of the team.

Combine this with our hardwired fear of losing social status, and it's easy for us to see performing new things in front of unfamiliar people as equivalent to the first round of the *American Idol* talent competition. Either we will "shock and awe" our audience and the YouTube video of our performance will get millions of hits, or we will get three X's and walk off stage in disgrace. No pressure there.

Psychologist Heidi Grant Halvorson argues that over time those of us with a "talent is mostly fixed" mindset come to worry a lot about how we will perform in front of others, and enter new situations with a primary focus on "being good."[3] We fear making mistakes or doing anything that might make us look bad.

Unfortunately, an excessive focus on being good has all kinds of consequences. If we're truly a beginner at something, we're nervous because our initial performance might reveal our lack of natural talent and hurt both our short- and long-term social status. If we think that others expect us to have some ability already, it's even worse. Then we worry about revealing ourselves as a fraud or impostor. Either way, we enter new situations with a huge amount of performance anxiety.

Researchers have found that a "talent is mostly fixed" mindset and an excessive focus on being good can cause us to:[4]

- Be too stressed about performing to really enjoy the new experience.
- Worry too much about proving ourselves.
- Try to be flawless and perfect (which often causes us to make even more mistakes).
- Become discouraged and give up more quickly.
- Never try something new in the first place (if we think we'll initially look bad doing it).

Sadly, we're often unintentionally taught to adopt a "being good" mindset, too. Carol Dweck and other researchers have shown that parents and teachers frequently praise children with comments like "you're so smart!" or "you are really good at this kind of thing." Unfortunately, we can infer from this praise that intelligence and talent are things we *have* rather than things we *develop* through practice and effort.[5] All is well until we attempt to do something that we're not really good at right away.

Fortunately, these researchers have also found that if we can shift our mindset from "being good" to "getting better," we can dramatically reduce the amount of performance anxiety we have in new situations.

REDUCE PERFORMANCE ANXIETY WITH
A "GETTING BETTER" MINDSET

An alternative strategy is to approach new situations with the belief that:

- Your talent is not fixed but can be developed and improved through learning and practice.
- Your first performance is not the "Big Reveal" of your natural talent but just the initial performance of somebody new.
- When you're new, nobody expects you to be perfect (or the complete expert).
- You'll make a better first impression if you focus on "getting better" rather than on "being good."

Carol Dweck, Heidi Grant Halvorson, and other researchers have shown that shifting our focus from "being good" to "getting better" has many benefits. If you don't automatically see your early mistakes and stumbles as the "Big Reveal" of your underlying talent, you're less worried about making them. You're also more likely to persist through initial difficulties and have more confidence in your ultimate mastery.

Improvement and the Power of "Getting Better"

Psychologist Lisa Blackwell and her colleagues demonstrated the power of this "getting better" mindset by examining one of the hardest newcomer transitions of all—seventh graders entering junior high school. They found that students who entered junior high with a "talent is not fixed" mindset and a focus on learning significantly improved their math grades over the next two years. In contrast, students who felt that math talent was mostly fixed tended to focus on achieving and performing in class and saw no improvement.

More important, the researchers also found they could significantly improve the math performance of under-achieving students by *teaching* them about the improvability of talent and the power of a learning-oriented, "getting better" mindset.[6] Other researchers have found similar results with other kinds of newcomer performances, including business negotiations.[7]

Exciting Challenges as the Benefits of "Getting Better"

Another benefit of a "getting better" mindset is that we tend to approach new situations as interesting challenges and exciting learning opportunities rather than stress-inducing tests of our natural abilities. According to Harvard University psychologist Alison Wood Brooks, this can actually help us take advantage of our anxiety and perform better.

In a series of experiments involving everything from solving math problems to public speaking and karaoke singing, she found something interesting. People who were told to repeat the phrase "I am excited" before performing the task in front of others did much better than people who were told to repeat the phrase "I am calm."

Upon further analysis, she discovered that those who repeated the phrase "I am excited" tended to approach the new task with an *opportunity*-oriented mindset, while those who repeated the phrase "I am calm" tended to approach the new task with a *threat*-oriented mindset, and that impacted performance. Once again, mindset matters.[8]

The Benefits of Not Focusing on "Being Good"

If you move away from a focus on performing and "being good," you will start to recognize that your initial performance is likely your first of many performances in front of your new group members, and that it will be viewed and evaluated by others in the context of your newness and "beginner-ness." In the end, your performance is only one way in which others get to know you.

In other words, the long-term social risk of your initial performance is probably much less than a "being good" mindset (and our prehistoric brains) would lead you to think.

What "Getting Better" Looks Like from the Other Side

Finally, when you focus on "getting better" rather than "being good," you will find you often behave in ways that make a positive impression on others. This includes:

- Showing respect (by asking for help and feedback).
- Demonstrating humility (by acknowledging that you still have more to learn).
- Avoiding highly competitive behavior (by focusing on learning than performing).

Think back to situations in which you've been the experienced, skilled veteran of the group. When you interact with newcomers and relative beginners:

- Do you automatically assume their first performance is the best they can ever do?
- Do you expect them to perform flawlessly right away?
- How does it make you feel if they come to you for help and advice? Or, alternatively, how does it make you feel if they join the group trying to compete and "beat" you?
- Who do you respect more—someone who tries hard or someone who tries to look good?

Overall, approaching new situations with a learning-oriented, "getting better" mindset can help create a positive first impression that will make it easier to gain the trust, respect, and productive relationships you need to be successful and happy.

THINK LIKE A SCIENTIST: GETTING TO "GETTING BETTER"

Let's explore a variety of strategies and approaches to help reduce your anxiety and reluctance to perform new things in front of unfamiliar people. Overall, the goal is to:

- Approach new situations with a learning-oriented, "getting better" mindset.
- Try your best while avoiding slipping back into a performance-oriented, "being good" mindset.

One of the best ways to ensure you actually shift your focus from "being good" to "getting better" is to approach new performances like a scientist instead of an *American Idol* contestant. This means approaching new performances with a focus on learning over performing, as experiments rather than exams or tests, with curiosity instead of competitiveness, and as an interesting challenge instead of something stressful to "get through."

Adopting a scientist's mindset can also help you "step outside yourself" and think about your upcoming performance (and the emotions it is generating) with a bit more detachment and objectivity. Once you start performing, a scientist's mindset can also help you realistically evaluate the results of your "experiment" and reflect upon your performance in ways that don't automatically trigger negative emotions like frustration, shame, and embarrassment.

Consider What You Are Really Trying to Achieve

One of the first questions you should ask yourself as you enter new situations is what you're really trying to gain from your upcoming performance. Why are you doing this? How will it bring you energy?

A "being good" mindset predisposes us to focus on maximizing and maintaining our social status. As a result, we often subconsciously assume that our primary goal is to:

- Impress others.
- Get ahead.
- Gain acceptance.

But in many new group situations, what we really want is often simply to:

- Get things done.
- Try and learn something new and challenging.
- Achieve personal and group goals.
- Have fun with others.

If dazzling and impressing the people around you isn't your primary objective, why allow yourself to think and act like it is? Of course, there are sometimes high-stakes, make-or-break performance situations in which you really want to impress others with your abilities. But these are often much more rare and unusual than our cave-dwelling brains lead us to believe.

Consider What's New and Challenging About What You're Doing

Once you clearly identify your performance goal, it's helpful to define exactly what is new and challenging about what you're trying to do. What causes us to be nervous in new performances is often one or more of the following situations:

- New roles and responsibilities
- New tasks requiring new skills and knowledge

- Unfamiliar processes and procedures
- New (or uncertain) social norms

Recognize that in most new situations, we perform a mix of the familiar and unfamiliar. For example, in your first job you may find your new role and the tasks, skills, and knowledge it requires to be relatively new. But the job is likely based on communication, teamwork, and problem-solving skills—all things that you've experienced in school and performed your entire life.

If you decide to learn a foreign language and take a French class, the French vocabulary and grammar may be new. But you're quite familiar with the role of being a student, and the processes and norms that typically occur in classrooms. So, separate what's new and challenging about the situation from what's familiar and easy. Often that can help reduce the size of the challenge and reduce your anxiety.

Consider What You Can Reasonably Expect from Your Initial Performance

It's not surprising that we're often predisposed to enter new situations with the subconscious desire to perform as well as established, high-status people. As a result, it's easy for us to create overly high expectations for our initial performance.

Obviously, you want to do your best, but based on your current knowledge and abilities, what's a reasonable expectation of your initial performance? If you're truly a beginner, can you really expect to perform as well as an expert? If you're new to a group, should you really assume you already have the knowledge and skill to flawlessly perform your new role?

One way to approach this issue is to think about something that *you're already really good at*. Then ask yourself the following questions:

- How would you expect a total beginner to perform this?
- What kinds of mistakes and stumbles would a beginner likely make?
- What kinds of things would you expect a newcomer *not* to know right away?

Armed with this perspective, now think about *your* upcoming performance as a newcomer or relative beginner and apply similar questions:

- What is a reasonable expectation of your initial performance?
- What are the kind of mistakes and stumbles you're likely to make?
- What are the kinds of things that you will likely not know about right away?

Depending on the situation, a reasonable expectation of your performance can vary widely, but this process can at least help you avoid a subconscious expectation of expert, flawless, perfection. Put on your scientist's hat and make a reasonable prediction of your performance, not what your genes, "being good" mindset, and ego would like you to do. For example, here are some reasonable expectations for beginning performances in a variety of newcomer situations:

1. Make the business presentation with a few blunders, and respond to one or two questions with "I don't know" or "I'll have to get back to you on that."
2. Have to rewrite and revise the report two or three times before it's ready for broad company distribution.
3. Hit several bad shots and lose six balls during your first round of golf.
4. Strum along, but not sing or take a solo, the first time you're in a music jam.

4. Go back to the hardware store at least three times before you have everything you need to wallpaper your bedroom.

Calculate the True Risk to Your Social Status

One effective way to overcome your fear of failure and social rejection is to put on your scientist's hat and evaluate the probability that your initial mistakes and stumbles will actually lead to a major loss in social status. In most cases, the risk is much lower than your "being good" mindset would lead you to think.

A lot of things have to happen before your initial, less-than-perfect performance has an impact on your social standing. In order for your initial performance to affect your social status, others have to:

- Pay attention to your performance.
- Notice your mistakes, hesitations, and general nervousness.
- Attribute them to your lack of natural talent (and not the fact that you're new or a beginner).
- Decide your less-than-stellar performance really matters to them.
- Respond in ways that impact your social status and group acceptance.

QUESTIONS TO ASK YOURSELF

Will they pay attention to my performance? Your performance in new situations will only impact your social status and success if people pay attention to that performance in the first place. Often you're just one of many people performing at the same time, not a solo act on a visible stage. Others around you are more likely preoccupied with their own thoughts, anxieties, and performances. While they might be aware of your presence, they often don't have the need, desire, or incentive to pay serious attention to what you're doing.

Will they notice my mistakes? Even if they pay attention to your performance, is it likely that they will actually notice your mistakes or make the mental effort to judge your performance? Social psychologists have repeatedly shown that:

- We tend to notice our own mistakes much more than other people do.
- Others often lack the knowledge or expertise to know a mistake when they see it.
- A mistake is often a discrepancy between intended and actual performance. If others don't know your intentions, how will they know if you made a mistake?

Will they attribute my mistakes to a lack of talent rather than that I am new? Even if others realize that you made mistakes, you'll only make a bad first impression if they attribute your performance to something other than the fact that you're new or a beginner. Often you can help ensure they attribute your performance to your newness by letting them know in advance that:

"I'm new to this."
"This is my first time."
"I've never tried this before."
"I'm a little nervous."

Will they care? Will they respond in ways that impact my status and success? Even if they conclude that you're an incompetent idiot, their opinion really has no impact on you unless they respond in ways that actually affect your social status or acceptance in a group. Suppose you make a spectacular fall on the ski slope and some strangers conclude you're an awful skier. Their opinion really has no effect on you unless they either convince people you care about that you're unworthy, or they ski over and try to kick you off the mountain. What's the chance of either of those happening?

We are often predisposed to interpret other peoples' actions as a negative reaction to our performance. For example, if someone yawns during our business presentation, we often interpret that as boredom instead of tiredness. If someone walks out of our presentation, we might automatically assume that they were disgusted with our performance, rather than that they had a sudden urge to go to the bathroom. We also tend to fixate on negative feedback, and concentrate on the one person who yawns or walks out rather than all the others who are attentive and interested in what we have to say.[9] Even if people respond negatively to our performance, what's the worst that can happen? Often the worst that can happen is some momentary embarrassment.

Preparing for the Performance:
Rehearsals and "Mental Walkthroughs"

One of the easiest ways to reduce your performance anxiety is to spend time preparing for your first performance. Often you can:

- Read and study about the new role, task, or skill *before* you attempt it. Between the Internet, books, and TV shows, you can probably find instruction and advice on just about anything.
- Talk to others who have experience doing the same thing and ask for advice.
- Watch other people perform (either live or on video) and vicariously put yourself in their shoes to imagine what it will be like.
- Script out your performance, especially opening lines.
- Rehearse your performance in private (or in front of people with whom you're comfortable performing).
- Do a mental walkthrough of your desired performance, imagining what you'll think, do, and say.
- Think through how you'll handle mistakes and failures.[10]

Whatever you do, the goal is to reduce your anxiety by effectively "pre-playing" your performance.

Meditation and Stress Relaxation Techniques

Some people find that meditation and other stress relaxation techniques (either before or during their newcomer performance) help them relax and shift their minds away from negative thoughts. There is nothing necessarily mystical about meditating, focused breathing, and muscle relaxation. Give it a try and see if it helps.[11]

Performing: What to Do in the Heat of the Moment

Often your anxiety starts to go away as soon as you start performing, but here are some things you can do in the heat of the moment to help keep the nervousness at bay:

- Focus on performing, not on your negative feelings and thoughts *about* performing.
- Adopt the scientist's perspective: step outside yourself and dispassionately observe your performance from time to time.
- Accept that you'll make a few mistakes, but don't dwell on them; concentrate on what you're doing now, not the mistake or misstep you made five minutes ago.
- Focus on what's interesting, challenging, and fun about what you're doing, not what is problematic and frustrating.
- If you can determine what you're not doing well, adjust your performance (as long as a mid-course change won't cause other problems).

Reflecting on Your Results: Dumb vs. Smart Failures

At the core of a "getting better" mindset is a willingness to reflect on your performance, accept both your successes and failures, and spend time thinking about how you can improve and do better next time.

One major difference between those with "being good" and "getting better" mindsets is how they think about and respond to feedback. Researchers have found through electroencephalography (EEG) studies that the brains of people who espouse a "getting better" mindset actually pay more attention to constructive feedback than those with a "being good" mindset.[12]

If you think about it, there are really two kinds of performance failures: *dumb failures* and *smart failures*. Dumb failures happen when your performance is poor because you weren't focused, or didn't plan well, or rushed through things. These kinds of failures aren't indicative of your true potential, and are usually somewhat preventable. If your dumb failures didn't kill you or cause permanent damage to your social status and reputation, then just accept what happened and challenge yourself to do better the next time.

Smart failures happen when you've planned as well as you could, tried your best, and the outcome still wasn't what you expected or desired. In this case, you might attribute your less-than-expected performance to your "beginner" status, or unexpected, emerging circumstances, or simply bad luck, rather than mistakes or errors you could have anticipated and corrected for in advance.

You'll be less anxious in new situations once you realize that if you learn something from your smart performance "failures," then they really weren't failures at all. In essence, you conducted a performance experiment—you tried your best to perform in a certain way, and it didn't match your aspirations. If you use what you learned to perform better the next time, then your initial performance wasn't really a failure; it was just a step on the road to mastery. Sounds a lot better that way, doesn't it?

HOW TO REFLECT, PRACTICE, AND GET BETTER AT "GETTING BETTER"

To become more comfortable and confident performing in new situations, you need to:

- Explore and uncover the reasons for your reluctance and anxiety.
- Mindfully observe how you think and act as you approach and perform new things.
- Identify strategies and approaches to shift from a "being good" to a "getting better" mindset.
- Find opportunities to experiment and practice across a variety of new performance situations.

Explore Your Anxiety or Reluctance to Perform New Things

Think back to past situations in which you've been anxious or reluctant to perform new things in front of unfamiliar people. What caused you to worry about performing?

- Fear of the negative consequences arising from mistakes (e.g., rework, delays, injury, etc.)?
- Fear of looking bad in front of other people?
- Fear of not meeting your own expectations and hurting your ego?
- Fear of the uncertainty and lack of control that comes with performing new, unfamiliar things?

Then look for patterns; for example:

- Does your reluctance vary by type of performance? Public speaking? Sports and exercise? Arts and creative performances?
- Does your anxiety vary by your current skill level? Are you more reluctant performing things when you're a total beginner? Or

when you think others already expect you to have a certain level of expertise?

- Are you more nervous performing in front of total strangers? Close acquaintances? Family and friends?
- Does the number of people you're performing in front of make a difference?

Reflecting on the types of new performance situations that cause you the most anxiety and reluctance can focus your attention and practice on the right things.

Mindfully Observe How You Perform (and Think about Performing) in New Situations

Since much of your anxiety and reluctance comes from assumptions, expectations, mindsets, and habits that you've developed over a lifetime of performing, by mindfully observing your thoughts and actions as you prepare to perform, as well as in the "heat of the moment," you can uncover whether you mostly have a "being good" or "getting better" mindset and what to do about it.

Over the next few weeks you will likely have the opportunity to perform new things in front of unfamiliar people. Mindfully observe your thoughts and emotions as you approach and prepare for the new situation. Ask yourself:

1. Am I spending more time thinking about the opportunity to try and learn something new, or on the possibility I'll make mistakes and look bad?
2. Do I see my upcoming performance as an interesting challenge or a test of my natural abilities?
3. Am I approaching this new performance situation like a scientist, student, or an *American Idol* contestant?

To help you approach performing with more of a "getting better" mind-set, next ask yourself the following:

- What am I trying to achieve? What do I want from this experience?
- What is new and challenging about this upcoming performance?
- Given my current knowledge and abilities, do I have a realistic expectation of my upcoming performance?
- Will others really notice, pay attention to, and truly care whether or not I perform well?
- What's the worst that can happen if they don't like what I do?
- How can I study, rehearse, and do "mental walkthroughs" to help me prepare for my performance?

As you start performing, observe your thoughts and emotions and ask yourself the following questions:

1. Did my anxiety continue while I performed, or did it mostly go away?
2. Am I spending more time thinking about how I'm doing, or how others might be thinking about how I'm doing?
3. When I make mistakes or encounter failure, do I think "I need to try harder" or "I'm just not good at this sort of thing"?
4. How do I respond to feedback? Do I seek or avoid it? Do I generally accept it or get defensive about it?
5. Do I spend time thinking about how I can do it better the next time?
6. Were my pre-performance anxieties justified? How can I incorporate that insight into my thinking the next time?

PRACTICE: PERFORM NEW THINGS IN FRONT OF UNFAMILIAR PEOPLE

The best way to become more comfortable and confident performing new things in front of unfamiliar people is simply to do it more often. For example:

- Seek out opportunities to practice performing things you're anxious about. If you are nervous about speaking in public, volunteer to make team presentations or join a Toastmaster's group.
- Try something completely new, and use the experience to explore how you approach and think about doing new things. Start a new hobby, take a class, or join a new club.

Often, what you learn in one performance situation can help you in others. For example, one newcomer I interviewed wanted to play banjo in bluegrass music jams, but was very intimidated by the prospect of performing in front of people. For the first two months he simply stayed in the "outer circle" and just strummed chords. He was afraid to take a solo, but then an opportunity presented itself:

"One night most people showed up late and there were just three or four people in the group. One person said, 'Why don't you give a break a try?' . . . I played pretty decently at home but in public I would fall apart. I played 'Cripple Creek,' and it was very humbling, I could tell I had a long way to go and needed to play a lot more."

Then he had a realization:

"But at that point I associated that feeling with the feeling I had when I spoke in public for the first time. Speaking in public and taking a break have a lot in common. It helped me realize that I would get better if I continued. In public speaking I learned I had to do enough of it to become comfortable. It's always this way when you are learning something."

Ultimately, the key to improving is to get out there and perform. As one newcomer I interviewed said, "You have to put yourself out there and do things before you can learn. How will you learn if you don't act?"

FIVE STEPS TO SUCCESSFULLY PERFORMING IN NEW SITUATIONS

In the end, success and happiness only come through action, and often this means performing new things in front of unfamiliar people. We're hardwired to fear the rejection and loss of social status that comes with making mistakes and having a less than optimal performance, and we also learn at an early age to focus more on "being good" than "getting better." This not only makes us anxious but it often causes us to make the very mistakes we most fear. However, you can become more comfortable and confident performing new things if you:

1. Adopt a scientist's mindset and focus on learning over performing.
2. Clearly identify what you want to achieve from your performance and what's new and challenging about it.
3. Assess your current abilities and create a reasonable expectation of your upcoming performance.
4. Realistically assess how much others will pay attention to your performance, and how much a less than perfect performance will actually impact you long term.
5. Mindfully reflect on how you approach performing in new situations, and adopt the strategies that help you focus on "getting better" over "being good."

Part 3

GIVING BACK AND GETTING OUT THERE

In this final section we'll explore ways to help others become more comfortable, confident, and successful newcomers, and provide you one last dose of advice and encouragement to help you push past your reluctance and seek out the new opportunities and experiences that can bring you the success and happiness you deserve.

TEN

GIVING BACK

Helping Others When They're New

In this chapter we will explore how we can assist other newcomers, and learn how to improve our ability to:

- Facilitate and develop the five newcomer skills in other people.
- Help newcomers become comfortable, confident, and accepted in the group.

So far, this book has been about how you can become a more confident, comfortable, and successful newcomer. But that is only half the picture. Once you're integrated, productive, and happy in your new group or organization, you have an obligation to "pay things forward" and find effective ways to welcome those who join after you.

We're now going to flip the five newcomer skills and explore how to help facilitate and develop these critical behaviors in others. These aren't the only elements of onboarding that you need to worry about when you welcome new people.[1] But by making it easier for newcomers to introduce themselves, remember names, ask questions, start relationships, and learn to perform new things, you can go a long way toward helping new arrivals become comfortable, confident, and accepted members, too.

REMEMBER WHAT IT'S LIKE TO BE NEW

As you think about onboarding others, it's important to realize that as an assimilated old-timer you likely have a very different mindset and perspective from what you had when you entered the group. This is especially true if you've been in the group a long time and have mastered the roles, skills, processes, and norms of the organization. It's amazing how quickly you can learn to take all these things for granted and forget what was like to be new.

Therefore, the first step toward facilitating these five newcomer skills in new arrivals is to put yourself back in a newcomer's mindset and to try to identify what is particularly challenging or frustrating about being new. Ask yourself, for example:

1. Does my group have unique or unusual roles, processes, or norms that are hard to figure out and learn?
2. Does being a productive member of the group require mastery of new skills that most newcomers don't have upon entry?
3. Are we particularly cliquish? Do current members have very strong friendships with each other and aren't looking for more relationships?
4. Is much of the critical information easily findable by newcomers, or is it locked in the heads of old-timers?

The more you can put yourself into a newcomer's mindset and see your organization as an outsider might view it, the better you can help onboard and facilitate these five newcomer behaviors in new people.

Ultimately, your goal is to create a safe, positive, welcoming environment where newcomers:

- Feel valued, accepted, and supported.
- Are willing to introduce themselves to new people.
- Learn and remember names but aren't too stressed-out if they happen to forget a name or two.
- Feel comfortable asking questions, especially of experts, leaders, teachers, coaches, and other key people.
- Build positive, productive relationships with people across the organization.
- Perform their new roles with confidence and with minimal anxiety.

HELP NEWCOMERS WITH INTRODUCTIONS

Over the past twenty years I've talked with hundreds of newcomers in dozens of companies, and I estimate that fewer than half of them have been really satisfied with the amount and quality of introductions they received when they joined their new organization. Given how important introductions are to asking questions, building relationships, and performing, don't assume that newcomers are comfortable introducing themselves. Not only should you facilitate initial introductions, you should do it in a way that gives the newcomer the confidence to start approaching others on his or her own.

Create an Introduction List

Before newcomers even arrive, make a list of the key people they need to meet in order to become productive, successful, integrated members of the organization. Think beyond their initial group members to include key support staff, administrators, managers, experts, coaches, and those they will likely run into as they engage in the group's activities.

Let Everyone Know the Newcomer is Coming

Facilitate newcomers' entry by announcing their arrival to everyone on the list. Give a little background about the new members and explain their initial roles. If appropriate, pre-arrange meetings with key people, or better yet, let these critical resources know they will be contacted soon by new arrivals. If newcomers know that others are ready and willing to meet them, it makes their initial approach and request that much easier.

One newcomer expressed his appreciation this way:

> "[My boss] said to them, 'I have a new employee and I'd like you to sit down and share what you do and answer his questions.' He basically prepared them in advance so I wasn't calling them out of the blue. This was very useful."

Make High-Quality Introductions in Small Doses

When the newcomers arrive, give them the introduction list and then connect them to those people they need to interact with right away. Try to make high-quality introductions in small doses, rather than rapid-fire, rushed introductions to everyone who happens to be around.

Introductions are essential onboarding events. They help jump-start relationships and provide the "permission slip" for future interactions. Introductions also create first impressions for both the newcomer and the person being introduced.

Use the opportunity of the formal introduction to:

- Explain their respective roles and how these roles are connected.
- Say nice things about both parties.
- Identify any common interests, experiences, or connections that might help jump-start their relationship.
- Ask the old-timers to give the newcomer advance permission to approach and ask questions.

One newcomer was really pleased with this approach:

"It was kind of cool because every time I got introduced to someone, [my boss] had something good to say about me—either that I was from [university], or that I was really bright, or that I came highly recommended."

Create Opportunities for Old-timers to Approach Newcomers

While most newcomers prefer being introduced to their new colleagues, they also appreciate it when strangers proactively approach them. For example, one newcomer said:

"In past companies I was often really nervous at first. I didn't feel comfortable after two or three days there but I did here. I was greeted and people came by and welcomed me on board. With other companies it took months to meet everyone and become friendly with them."

Ideally, organizations have social norms that encourage old-timers to seek out and introduce themselves to newcomers. But there are also many creative ways to help jump-start these connections. Through my interviews I've heard of organizations that:

- Place a box of doughnuts or bowl of candy at the newcomer's desk (and let the rest of the organization know the food is there).
- Attach a balloon to the newcomer's desk to signal the person's arrival (and encourage everyone to stop by and say hi).
- Put up a welcome sign at the entrance announcing the newcomer's arrival, along with a picture, brief bio, and work location.

Revisit and Expand the List

After a few days or weeks (whatever seems appropriate), meet with newcomers and review their initial introduction lists. Find out who the newcomers haven't met yet, and either make or facilitate introductions.

HELP NEWCOMERS REMEMBER NAMES

When it comes to remembering names, newcomers are at a disadvantage. Old-timers only have to remember one or two new names, while newcomers have to remember dozens if not more. Your goal should be to create an environment where newcomers:

- Are reassured that the organization doesn't expect them to remember and recall everyone's name in the first few days.
- Are repeatedly exposed to names (so they learn them).
- Have access to the names and pictures of those they have met (in case they forget).
- Aren't too stressed out if they can't recall a name in the heat of the moment.

Provide Newcomers with Lists and Organizational Charts

When newcomers arrive, provide them with lists that can help them learn, memorize, and recall names of the people they eventually meet. Start with the introduction list, but include organizational charts, membership rosters—anything that can be helpful.

Some organizations put up names and pictures of members on websites, walls, or bulletin boards. This is a great way for people to connect names with faces, and it provides an anonymous way for people to rediscover a name they've forgotten.

Nametags and Other Identifiers

Most newcomers I've interviewed appreciate the initial benefits that come from having everyone consistently wear nametags. Nametags (and to a lesser extent cubicle and office door signs) help ensure that newcomers are repeatedly exposed to names, and is a simple, safe, low-cost way to recall a name if the newcomer forgets it.

The only potential downside of nametags is when they become a substitute for memory. If newcomers come to rely on nametags as their primary recall mechanism (instead of really learning and committing the names to long-term memory), then newcomers will have real problems if they meet people in situations in which they aren't wearing nametags.

Encourage Colleagues to Help Newcomers Learn Names

You can also help new people learn names by encouraging your colleagues to:

- Restate their name at the end of all introductions.
- Reintroduce themselves the first few times they interact with new arrivals (to increase repetition and learning).
- Start meetings and group activities with a round of introductions (if they think the new people haven't met everyone in the room).

FACILITATE NEWCOMER QUESTION-ASKING

Often the quickest, best way to help newcomers become productive, satisfied members is ensure that new arrivals:

- Know who to ask for information and advice (or at least who to ask first).

- Become comfortable approaching and interrupting experts and key resources with their questions.
- Come to realize that asking questions has relatively low social risk.

There are several things that we can do to help facilitate proactive question-asking.

Provide a List of Resources

Once again, lists are important. Giving newcomers a starting list of key resources can help them identify and target the right people for information. Introducing new people to those on the list can also give newcomers implicit permission to approach them later with questions.

But remind newcomers that you're only giving them a starting list. As they interact with others and ask questions, they will undoubtedly uncover other people who can help them achieve their goals. Encourage them to expand the list as they meet new people, and ask others who they should seek out next.

Direct Newcomers to Online Resources

Don't assume the newcomers will find the most critical information stored on organizational websites, staff directories, and company databases. As one newcomer said, "Don't make it so much like a treasure hunt." Provide an initial list of the most useful online resources that can help jump-start their productivity.

Find Newcomers (or Help Them Find) a Buddy

All newcomers need at least one "buddy" who they feel completely comfortable approaching with their miscellaneous "newbie" questions. Ideally, these buddy relationships emerge naturally, but sometimes it can help to identify and formally designate a buddy in advance. The best buddies are often those who have been there long enough to be helpful to the newcomer, but not so long that they haven't forgotten what it's like to be new. Here's how one newcomer described the benefits of having a buddy:

> "They assigned a buddy who showed me around. She took me to lunch and said if I had any questions I could ask her. She still answers my questions. . . . It's good because you immediately have one friend that you can ask for help or ask them where to go for help."

Check in Periodically

Don't forget to stop by from time to time and ask newcomers if they have questions. For newcomers who are reluctant to bother other people with questions, this can be a welcome event. You can also encourage team members and other key resources to do the same.

Revisit and Review their Resource List

Once they've been there a while, ask the newcomers for a list of people they've approached for help and advice. Look for gaps or key people they haven't tapped yet, and facilitate introductions.

Refer Newcomers to Others to Help Build Their Network

Once newcomers find someone who is approachable and helpful, they will sometimes rely on this person too much and not build the full network of relationships they need to be successful. If you find yourself becoming that chronic "go-to" person, and you feel it's starting to become counterproductive, don't answer their next question. Instead, refer the newcomer to someone else, and if necessary help make the connection.

**Encourage Old-timers to Accept Interruptions
from Newcomers**

The best organizations build a helping culture where old-timers expect
and are willing to be interrupted by newcomers. One manager I interviewed said:

> "I would sit down with the other employees and make it clear that
> the new guy would be asking them questions. . . . Let the old-timers
> know that the new person needs help and they shouldn't get an-
> noyed if they are approached with questions."

If newcomers approach group members and discover that most are
approachable, interruptible, and helpful, it will give them the confidence
to seek out even more people. As one newcomer said:

> "I would ramp up more quickly if it was easier to communicate with
> people. If I knew my place and how interruptible people were, and
> if people said things like 'bother me any time' so I know I can go ask
> them questions."

HELP NEWCOMERS START RELATIONSHIPS

Most newcomers are not hermits or curmudgeons. They want to develop relationships, not only to help them succeed but also to feel connected to and accepted by the organization. Researchers have repeatedly
shown that newcomers who build a large, diverse network of relationships are more productive, more satisfied, and more loyal to the organization.[2]

You can't guarantee that newcomers will develop the relationships
they need to be successful and happy, but you can help create opportunities for new people to meet and socialize with people across the organization. Besides facilitating individual introductions, here are a few ideas:

Create Official Newcomer Welcoming Activities

The arrival of new members gives you both the opportunity and the justification to connect them to existing members through a variety of official events and activities. One of the most common approaches is the welcome lunch, though I've also heard about welcome breakfasts, dinners, coffee breaks, or after-hours drinks.

Some organizations also have ceremonies or rituals where the newcomer is formally introduced and welcomed by group members. Over the years I've interviewed organizations that publicly present newcomers with t-shirts, hats, coffee mugs, name plates, or other symbolic representations of the group. Other organizations have newcomers add their name to a wall containing the signatures of all current and former employees.

Sometimes these ceremonies and rituals are stand-alone events, while other times they are made part of regularly scheduled meetings or group activities. Either way, the specific details of these welcome lunches, ceremonies, and rituals are probably less important than having an event that:

- Everyone attends and enjoys.
- Truly welcomes the newcomers to the organization.
- Signifies the importance of the newcomers' arrival.
- Makes the newcomers feel valued and accepted.
- Helps jump-start new relationships.

Regular Social Events
Often, helping newcomers start new relationships is simply a numbers game—the more opportunities you give them to meet and socialize with old-timers, the more likely these initial conversations will lead to acquaintances and friendships. There are endless possibilities:

- End-of-week, holiday, and birthday parties
- Celebrations of project milestones and group success

- Bowling, golf, or other group excursions
- Retreats and team-building events
- Employee coffee breaks

Again, the specific nature and details of the activity are probably less important than ensuring that new people meet and socialize with others during the event. As one newcomer said:

"This really helped me with being new, and was a great start. . . . In those gatherings I was able to find out what things were going on in the organization, what I had in common with other people."

Invite Newcomers to Join the "Lunch Bunch"
Through my interviews I've discovered that one area of stress and anxiety for newcomers is lunch, especially if people in the organization regularly go out to lunch together. While existing members often have to interact with new people in the course of group activities, there is nothing mandatory about including them in the "lunch bunch." In a sense lunch can be one of the first litmus tests of acceptance a newcomer gets in an organization.

If your organization has "lunch bunches," make sure that newcomers get invited and quickly integrated into these daily lunch routines. Lunch is one of the best ways for newcomers to build relationships and ask questions outside of normal work activities. The same advice applies to organizations with regular group routines around coffee breaks and after-activity socializing.

Periodically Review Newcomers' Relationship Networks

It's wise to periodically check in with new arrivals to:

- See who they have met and how these relationships have progressed over time.

- Identify who they still need to meet to become more productive and integrated.
- Help facilitate additional introductions and connections.

Your goal is to ensure that newcomers are building the initial connections they need to be successful, as well as gain the confidence to proactively approach and start relationships with additional people over time.

HELP NEWCOMERS PERFORM NEW THINGS

Newcomers are often anxious about performing new roles, tasks, and skills in front of unfamiliar groups. If they are total beginners, they fear the embarrassment and potential rejection that comes with performing more poorly than established, experienced members. If they have represented themselves as accomplished experts during the hiring or application process, they fear being exposed as impostors or frauds. As an old-timer, your goal is to help new arrivals adopt a learning-oriented, "getting better" mindset over a performance-oriented, "being good" mindset. More specifically, you want to create the conditions where newcomers:

- Feel comfortable trying and performing new things.
- Don't stress over the inevitable stumbles and mistakes.
- Are willing to ask for and receive feedback.
- Gain proficiency and confidence over time.

There are several things you can do to make this happen, including the following:

Clearly Explain Their New Role

One of the greatest sources of newcomer anxiety is role uncertainty. If new people aren't sure what they are supposed to do, it's hard for them be confident in their initial performances. Researchers also have shown that when newcomers clearly understand their new role, they tend to have higher productivity, greater satisfaction, and increased commitment to the group.[3]

Make sure that in early conversations you explain their new roles and responsibilities as well as:

- What tasks and skills are required
- What a typical newcomer performance looks like
- What resources are available to help them succeed

Give Them an Achievable Challenge

To help newcomers become less anxious performers, you also want to give them an initial set of goals and associated tasks that are:

- Engaging and interesting (to promote learning)
- Challenging but achievable (to build confidence)
- Completed with others (to build relationships)

Achievable challenges matter. Researchers at AT&T found that the amount of challenge in new hires' initial assignments predicted promotion levels and career success years later.[4] As one manager said:

"A lot does go back to the first project. The first project if possible should be very compartmentalized and should not necessarily be an easy one but should provide a nice introduction to the system and be one where you don't need to understand the entire ball of wax to get it done. You want them to do something that gives them confidence and a feel for what's there."

Provide Timely and Constructive Feedback

Many newcomers are nervous in new situations because they have a hard time judging their own efforts. Providing timely and constructive feedback can reduce performance anxiety by helping newcomers:

- Notice and evaluate their true (as opposed to imagined) performance.
- Identify easy ways for them to quickly improve their technique and see real progress.
- Avoid initial expectations of flawless, expert performance (especially with newcomer perfectionists).
- Continue with their improvement efforts (especially through initial stumbles).

Newcomers also appreciate offers to help them rehearse, practice, and prepare for upcoming performances.

Ask Questions to Promote a "Getting Better" Mindset

One of the best things you can do to help newcomers become confident, comfortable performers is to "coach" them by asking questions that:

- Promote mindful reflection.
- Expose counterproductive assumptions, habits, and expectations.
- Encourage practice and recalibration.

There is no magic formula for a good "coaching" session, but often you simply need to ask a mixture of the following questions:

1. What were you trying to accomplish?
2. How do you think it went?

3. Did it go better or worse than you expected?
4. What went well?
5. What can you do better next time?
6. Can you identify or create opportunities to practice?
7. How can I help?

The goal is to help newcomers reflect upon their initial experiences and see the benefits of adopting a practice-based, learning-oriented, "getting better" mindset.

SEVEN STEPS TO SUCCESSFULLY HELPING OTHERS WHEN THEY ARE NEW

Once we're integrated, productive, and satisfied members of our group we have the obligation and responsibility to help welcome and onboard new arrivals. There are many things we can do to help facilitate self-introductions, name-remembering, question-asking, relationship-building, and performing, including:

1. Providing lists of key people
2. Announcing the newcomer's arrival and facilitating introductions
3. Explaining new roles and tasks
4. Finding (or helping find) a buddy
5. Hosting welcome lunches, ceremonies, and other social events
6. Reviewing and helping expand the newcomer's network of relationships
7. Providing feedback and coaching

Overall, your goal is to help create a safe, welcoming environment where newcomers learn to confidently perform their new role and develop the relationships they need to be successful and happy.

ELEVEN

GET OUT THERE AND SUCCEED

In this final chapter we will review the most important strategies for becoming a more comfortable, confident newcomer and see how others have succeeded using them when they were new. I also include some parting advice on how to get started and maintain the focus you need to see real progress.

TO BE HAPPY, TRY SOMETHING NEW

Social psychologist Sonja Lyubomirsky has spent years trying to understand what makes people happy, and, more important, how to sustain that happiness over time. Through dozens of studies, she and her colleagues have concluded that about 50 percent of a person's happiness is determined by his or her genes—we're partly hardwired for a certain level of happiness.

But we control the other 50 percent. The researchers found that about 40 percent of our happiness is based on our current activities and 10 percent is based on our current circumstances. The challenge is that the amount of happiness we get from specific activities and situations tends to go down over time.[1] We lose interest. We get bored. Everything is too predictable.

Lyubomirsky and her colleagues therefore suggest that the key to sustainable happiness lies in trying new things:

> What are the most general recommendations for increasing happiness suggested by our model? Simply, that happiness-seekers might be advised to find new activities to become engaged in—preferably activities that fit their values and interests.[2]

You can find or create new activities in many ways. You can:

- Seek a job that challenges you with new roles, tasks, and skill demands.
- Learn a new hobby.
- Take on a new sport.
- Join new clubs and volunteer organizations.
- Move to new cities or travel to new locations.

In almost every one of these situations, you are a newcomer to something or somebody. And your willingness to put yourself into new experiences often depends on how comfortable and confident you are with introducing yourself, remembering names, asking questions, starting relationships, and performing new things in front of unfamiliar people.

If you've come this far, you've spent this entire book understanding why you get anxious in new situations and in exploring ways to get better at these five key newcomer skills. With each skill, real improvement only comes through reflection and practice.

So now you face a choice. You can finish this book and move onto other things, taking away, I hope, one or two insights that will make you less anxious in new situations. Maybe you'll see a little improvement in your ability to introduce yourself, remember names, and so on. Or, you can make a *real commitment today* to do the reflection and practice required to see real improvement in one or more of these five newcomer skills. This doesn't mean that you have to drop everything in your life and focus entirely on becoming a better newcomer. You just need to make an honest commitment to:

- Imagine the kind of newcomer you'd like to become (and how that will make you more successful and happy).
- Pick one or more newcomer skills whose improvement will help you become your ideal newcomer.
- Pay attention to your thoughts, emotions, and actions when performing these skills over the next few weeks.
- Reference this book (and your own ideas) to identify strategies, approaches, and techniques that can help you improve your confidence, comfort, and ability.
- Try out these new strategies, approaches, and techniques and see what works best for you.
- Look for opportunities to practice (and reflect).
- Periodically assess your progress (and get feedback from others).
- Keep at it until you become the newcomer you desire to be.

There are several things you can do to increase your chances for success.

1. *Make a public commitment.* You're much more likely to persist with reflection and practice if you tell others about your newcomer goals. They can provide help, encouragement, and advice, and you'll feel more obligated to live up to your promises. As one newcomer I interviewed put it:

   > "Get a mentor or friend to try it with you, or talk with people who have done it before. Talk to somebody about it and then get them to encourage you to do it. Find a designated

person who you trust that will ask, 'What is holding you back? Go do it!'"

2. *Acknowledge your Stone Age brain.* Recognize that you've inherited a predisposition to be anxious in new situations, and likely have learned at an early age to be nervous around strangers. Accept it and move on.

3. *The worst-case scenario rarely happens.* Most of the time the failures and social rejections we fear in new situations never happen. Often the worst-case scenario is just a brief moment or two of embarrassment.

4. *Put yourself in others' shoes.* If you're nervous about approaching and interacting with others, ask yourself how you would think and react if the roles were switched.

5. *Approach new situations as experiments, not tests.* Try to approach newcomer experiences as experiments and learning opportunities rather than make-or-break tests of your performance abilities. Focus on "getting better" instead of "being good."

6. *Give and seek energy.* Spend less time trying to impress others and more time showing real interest in who they are and what they do. People like being around people who are positive and give them energy. But don't neglect your own needs—seek out activities that also bring *you* energy.

7. *Write things down.* Most of us have relatively poor memories. Getting things down on paper (or onto your computer) can help you recall important information when you need it.

8. *Be patient.* You're attempting to change habits, assumptions, and expectations you've had your entire life. You'll probably see rapid improvement in some areas, and experience slow going in others. Be patient and trust that with reflection and practice you'll ultimately see real progress.

THE POWER OF PUTTING YOURSELF OUT THERE

Remember that your ultimate goal isn't simply becoming a more comfortable, confident newcomer. It's the success and happiness you find when you're more willing to seek out and take advantage of new opportunities and experiences.

For example, one newcomer I interviewed dreamed for years about creating a one-man theatrical and musical show about his favorite country music artist. He had no acting experience, and was extremely nervous about putting himself out there and taking acting lessons at the local community college: "I'm shy by nature and pretty introverted. When I told people I was going to take acting classes, they said 'You're going to do what?!'"

When I asked him how his first few classes went, he said "awful," adding:

> "At the community college about 95 percent of the class are nineteen- and twenty-year-olds, and at the time I was fifty and only one or two others were my age or older. Being asked to perform in front of the class by myself was tough. I kept jumping back and forth from foot to foot and couldn't keep my hands still. They kept having to tell me to plant my feet."

I asked him about his emotions in this new situation:

> "Fear was a big one. Like most I would probably pick death over public speaking. I felt a lot of self-doubt. I didn't know if I would be able to master this or bluff so that other people would be interested. There were a lot of experienced, trained actors who could play off other people on stage. I was very reluctant to open up and let that happen."

But he persisted, and had the courage to try out for a small part in the play the class performed at the end of the semester. His worst fears about performing never materialized, and he kept moving forward:

> "After that first show in April I auditioned at the local community theater group. A friend suggested that I show up. It turned out it was a musical, and they needed warm bodies so they thrust a songbook in my hand and we began rehearsing. I got to experience working with a choreographer and with coaches for singing."

Performing on stage in front of strangers was still intimidating, but he started to feel better about doing it:

> "I was part of the ensemble, so there were no solo parts, but I did sing and dance. There was security in numbers. I felt very inadequate and didn't want to detract from the show, but I did OK."

As he continued to take classes and work on his one-man show, he gained the confidence to approach others, ask questions, and start new relationships:

> "I developed a whole new set of friends. I approached them about my project and asked for feedback and how I could refine my technique. I also ended up making contacts at two or three other community theaters. I developed friendships and contacts across a variety of venues."

Over the next few months, he continued to develop and revise his show, and when he was invited to perform it at a homeowner's association meeting: "I rehearsed it for weeks and got back in touch with my instructor who helped me prepare, and then did the 45-minute show in front of fifty people."

They gave him a standing ovation. He continued to develop and add material to the show and found opportunities to perform it before new audiences. He attributes much of his success to practice and persistence:

"But for me it's just been repetition and doing it and becoming more comfortable and more willing to open up. It's exciting to go out there and be well received in the role and respond to it."

He's proud of what he has created, but more important he's thrilled with the new relationships he has created in the process:

"Probably the biggest [benefit] is that it's opened me up to a whole new family. Before I had maybe two or three close friends I hung out with and now it's mushroomed to 75 or 100 people I connect with and interact with on a regular basis. It's totally changed my life."

CHANGE WILL HAPPEN: JUST GO FOR IT

In the end, nothing will change until you take action and put yourself out there. You'll always feel a little bit anxious when you're new, and some nervousness is actually a good thing (as it keeps you focused and alert). But you can become a more comfortable and confident newcomer, and use that confidence to seek out and embrace the new opportunities and experiences that can bring you the success and happiness you desire.

As one newcomer describes it:

"You have to get past who you are inside and take more chances. You'll only get used to something if you suck it up and try it. It's hard to get used to something unless you put yourself out there."

One newcomer I interviewed described being new as that first hill on a roller coaster ride. As you slowly get pulled higher and higher, you're both excited and nervous, both anticipating and dreading what will happen once you crest that first hill and scream down the other side. But once you're over the top and twisting and turning, the experience is fantastic, and when you come to a stop you're ready to jump out and do it again. The hardest part is having the courage to step into that roller coaster in the first place.

Another newcomer put it this way:

"The biggest and most beneficial thing is just to swallow the fear. . . . I've found the best times I've had have been when I forget about the fear and just did it. In new situations especially I've found that the amount of fear I've had [about trying something] is correlated with how happy I am after I've done it."

Some of our fear comes from the lack of control we often feel as we enter new situations. But the key is to push past that anxiety and take action. Another newcomer said this:

"I think success for a newcomer comes when they can put themselves out there in the situation where it's not in their sphere of influence, and have the confidence to do it. To embrace new situations is in some ways an act of bravery. But I find that after I've joined something I'm proud of myself for having made the effort."

YOU'RE NOT ALONE: EVERYONE MAKES MISTAKES

It's inevitable that as a newcomer and beginner you will likely stumble. Recognize that it's normal and expected. In most social situations you're not the only one who is anxious. One newcomer put it this way:

"Others probably feel the same way as you do. Put yourself out there and introduce yourself and take on new challenges. You really have nothing to lose. Sometimes it's really hard, but with new challenges you feel better after you do it. It's one more thing you've accomplished in your life."

In the end, the advice of one more newcomer I interviewed beautifully sums up the message of this book:

"Smile a lot. Imagine that other people are just as awkward. Don't focus on your fear, focus on theirs. Show them that you're interested in them. Be helpful and appreciative. Don't worry about being funny or entertaining, just be kind."

Put yourself out there, try new things, meet new people, and seek the success, energy, and joy you deserve. Have fun!

NOTES

CHAPTER 1: SUCCESS STARTS WITH BEING NEW

1. P. Ingram and M. W. Morris, "Do People Mix at Mixers?: Structure, Homophily, and the 'Life of the Party.'" *Administrative Science Quarterly* 52, no. 4 (2007): 558–85.
2. A press release of the survey results can be found at http://news.ladbrokes.com/en-gb/press-office/ladbrokes-commission-survey-to-coincide-with-chris-kamara-ad_116694.html.
3. M. Buckingham and C. Coffman, *First, Break All the Rules: What the World's Greatest Managers Do Differently* (New York: Simon & Schuster, 1999).
4. If you want advice on how to transition into new leadership roles, an excellent book is Michael Watkin's *The First Ninety Days* (Cambridge, MA: Harvard Business Review Press, 2013).

CHAPTER 2: ALWAYS A NEWCOMER

1. Over 94 percent of us participate in at least one out-of-class activity during high school; A. Duffet and J. Jonson, (2004) *All Work and No Play: Listening to What Kids and Parents Really Want From Out-of-School Time,* report commissioned by The Wallace Foundation, 2004, available at www.wallacefoundation.org/knowledge-center/after-school/key-research/Pages/All-Work-and-No-Play.aspx.
2. Bureau of Labor Statistics, "Number of Jobs Held, Labor Market Activity, and Earnings Growth Amount the Youngest Baby Boomers: Results from a Longitudinal Survey," news release USDL-12-1489, July 25, 2012, available at www.bls.gov/nls.
3. The Census Bureau made these estimates based on the 2007 American Community Survey (http://www.census.gov/acs/www/). How they calculated them is described at www.census.gov/hhes/migration/about/cal-mig-exp.html.
4. Pew Internet Research, "The Social Side of the Internet," report released on January 18, 2011, available at http://pewinternet.org/Reports/2011/The-Social-Side-of-the-Internet.aspx.
5. Pew Internet Research, "The Social Side of the Internet."

6. The National Ski Areas Association routinely publishes their Model for Growth report, which analyzes "first-timer conversion rates"; more info is available at www.nsaa.org/growing-the-sport/model-for-growth/model-for-growth-detailed/.

CHAPTER 3: NATURE AND NURTURE

1. R. Moreland, "Social Categorization and the Assimilation of 'New' Group Members," *Journal of Personality and Social Psychology* 48 (1985): 1173–90.
2. D. J. Nash and A. W. Wolfe, "The Stranger in Laboratory Culture," *American Journal of Sociology* 78 (1957): 399–417.
3. There is much debate about the exact group size of our prehistoric ancestors. Based on ethnographic studies of modern hunter-gatherer tribes, scientists estimate that groups were probably in the 30 to 50 range. See F. W. Marlowe, "Hunter-Gatherers and Human Evolution," *Evolutionary Anthropology: Issues, News, and Reviews* 14, no. 2 (2005): 54–67.
4. Evolutionary anthropologists estimate that for much of human history we lived in small, nomadic groups of close relatives who roamed around in a relatively limited area hunting game and gathering food. We were also loosely connected to other nearby hunter-gatherer groups, and perhaps shared a common culture (and later language) with maybe another 500 people in the area, sometimes getting together for ceremonies and celebrations. See S. Mithen, *After the Ice Age: A Global Human History, 20,000–5000 BC* (Cambridge, MA: Harvard University Press, 2004).
5. J. E. Pfeiffer, *The Emergence of Man,* 3rd ed. (New York: Harper & Row, 1978).
6. R. I. Dunbar, "Coevolution of Neocortical Size, Group Size and Language in Humans," *Behavioral and Brain Sciences* 16, no. 4 (1993): 681–94.
7. J. Barko, L. Cosmides, and J. Tooby, *The Adapted Mind: Evolutionary Psychology and the Generation of Culture* (New York: Oxford University Press, 1992).
8. P. J. Richerson and R. Boyd, (2005). *Not by Genes Alone: How Culture Transformed Human Evolution* (Chicago: University of Chicago Press, 2005).
9. Richerson and Boyd, *Not by Genes Alone,* 224.
10. I. M. Marks, *Fears, Phobias and Rituals* (New York: Oxford University Press, 1987).
11. E. Waters, L. Matas, and L. A. Sroufe, "Infants' Reactions to an Approaching Stranger: Description, Validation, and Functional Significance of Wariness," *Child Development* 46, no. 2 (1975): 348–56.
12. Marks, *Fears, Phobias and Rituals.*
13. "Utah Scout Feeling 'Good' After Ordeal," CNN, June 23, 2005, available at http://edition.cnn.com/2005/US/06/22/missing.scout/.
14. The U.S. Department of Justice conducted a study of children reported missing in 1999. Out of 800,000 reported incidents, they estimate that only 115 were abductions by complete strangers. Almost all abductions were by people known to the child. See A. J. Sedlak, D. Finkelhor, H. Hammer, and D. J. Schultz, *National Estimates of Missing Children: An Overview* (Washington, DC: Office of Juvenile Justice and Delinquency Prevention, 2002), retrieved from www.ncjrs.gov/pdffiles1/ojjdp/196465.pdf.
15. M. R. Leary, "Affiliation, Acceptance and Belonging," in *Handbook of Social Psychology,* ed. S. T. Fiske, D. T. Gilbert, and L. Gardner (New York: John Wiley, 2010), 864–97.
16. W. F. Allman, *The Stone Age Present: How Evolution Has Shaped Modern Life— from Sex, Violence, and Language to Emotions, Morals, and Communities* (New York: Simon & Schuster, 1994).
17. C. Barnard and T. Burk, "Dominance Hierarchies and the Evolution of 'Individual Recognition,'" *Journal of Theoretical Biology* 81, no. 1 (1979): 65–73.
18. S. Mithen, *After the Ice Age: A Global Human History, 20,000–5000 BC* (Cambridge, MA: Harvard University Press, 2004).
19. P. Seabright, *The Company of Strangers: A Natural History of Economic Life* (Princeton, NJ: Princeton University Press, 2004), 4.
20. R. Wright, *The Moral Animal: The New Science of Evolutionary Psychology* (New York: Pantheon Books, 1994), 38–39.

CHAPTER 4: THE POWER OF PRACTICE AND REFLECTION

1. There are several articles that provide a good overview of the science of deliberate practice, including K. A. Ericsson, "Deliberate Practice and Acquisition of Expert Performance: A General Overview," *Academic Emergency Medicine* 15, no. 11 (2008): 988–94; K. A. Ericsson, R. T. Krampe, and C. Tesch-Römer, "The Role of Deliberate Practice in the Acquisition of Expert Performance," *Psychological Review* 100, no. 3 (1993): 363–406; and K. A. Ericsson, M. J. Prietula, and E. T. Cokely, "The Making of an Expert," *Harvard Business Review* 85, nos. 7/8 (2007): 114–21.

2. R. P. Abelson, "Psychological Status of the Script Concept," *American Psychologist* 36 (1981): 715–29.

3. There has been extensive research on mental models, including that by P. N. Johnson-Laird, *Mental Models: Towards a Cognitive Science of Language, Inference, and Consciousness* (Cambridge, MA: Harvard University Press, 1983). See also D. Gentner and A. L. Stevens, *Mental Models* (New York: Psychology Press, 2014).

4. The term *self-fulfilling prophecy* was coined by Robert Merton, in his book *Social Theory and Social Structure* (New York: Free Press, 1968), 3. An overview of research in this area can be found in R. A. Jones, *Self-fulfilling Prophecies: Social, Psychological, and Physiological Effects of Expectancies* (Mahwah, NJ: Lawrence Erlbaum, 1977).

5. K. A. Ericsson, M. J. Prietula, and E. T. Cokely. "The Making of an Expert," *Harvard Business Review* 85, nos. 7/8 (2007): 114–21.

6. The 10,000-hour rule was popularized by Malcolm Gladwell in his best-selling book *Outliers: The Story of Success* (London: Penguin UK, 1986).

7. An overview of cognitive-behavioral therapy can be found in C. R. Brewin, "Theoretical Foundations of Cognitive-Behavior Therapy for Anxiety and Depression," *Annual Review of Psychology* 47 (1996): 33. There are dozens of good books on CBT, including W. T. O'Donohue and J. E. Fisher, *Cognitive Behavior Therapy: Core Principles for Practice* (Hoboken, NJ: John Wiley, 2012). Also see R. Branch and R. Willson, *Cognitive Behavioral Therapy for Dummies*, 2nd ed. (New York: John Wiley, 2010).

8. S. Suzuki, *Zen Mind, Beginner's Mind* (New York: Weatherhill, 1995).

9. There is some dispute over exactly when and by whom this model was created, but it's generally attributed to Noel Birch, a former employee of Gordon Training International. You can learn more about this competence model at http://www.gordontraining.com/free-workplace-articles/learning-a-new-skill-is-easier-said-than-done/.

10. The power of public commitment and other persuasion techniques are wonderfully described in the classic book by R. B. Cialdini, *Influence: The Psychology of Persuasion* (New York: HarperCollins, 2007).

CHAPTER 5: INTRODUCING YOURSELF

1. E. Dunn and M. Norton, "Hello, Stranger," *New York Times*, April 27, 2014, p. 1.

2. N. Epley and J. Schroeder, "Let's Make Some Metra Noise," *Chicago Tribune*, June 5, 2011, p. 16.

3. I. A. Youssouf, A. D. Grimshaw, and C. S. Bird, "Greetings in the Desert," *American Ethnologist* 3, no. 4 (1976): 797–824.

4. P. Post, A. Post, L. Post, and D. Post Senning, *Emily Post's Etiquette: Manners for a New World*, 18th ed. (New York: William Morrow, 2011).

5. Ibid., 17–18.

6. http://www.uncommonhelp.me/articles/conversation-starter-talk-to-strangers-with-ease/#sthash.0EbcLnlZ.dpuf.

CHAPTER 6: REMEMBERING NAMES

1. D. Carnegie, *How to Win Friends and Influence People* (New York: Pocket Books, 1981), 79.

2. R. S. Newman, "The Cocktail Party Effect in Infants Revisited: Listening to One's Name in Noise," *Developmental Psychology* 41, no. 2 (2005): 352–62.

3. D. P. Carmody and M. Lewis, "Brain Activation When Hearing One's Own and Others' Names," *Brain Research* 1116, no. 1 (2006): 153–58.

4. W. Staffen, M. Kronbichler, M. Aichhorn, A. Mair, and G. L. Mair, "Selective Brain Activity in Response to One's Own Name in the Persistent Vegetative State," *Journal of Neurology, Neurosurgery, and Psychiatry* 77 (2006): 1383–84.

5. G. W. Allport, *Pattern and Growth in Personality* (New York: Holt, Reinhart, and Winston, 1963), 117.

6. D. J. Howard, C. Gengler, and A. Jain, "What's in a Name?: A Complimentary Means of Persuasion," *Journal of Consumer Research* 22, no. 2 (1995): 200–11.

7. B. W. Pelham, M. C. Mirenberg, and J. T. Jones, "Why Susie Sells Seashells by the Seashore: Implicit Egotism and Major Life Decisions," *Journal of Personality and Social Psychology* 82, no. 4 (2002): 469–87.

8. I have chosen to use the traditional three-system memory framework by Atkinson and Shiffrin to explain why we are bad at remembering names. More recent MRI studies have shown that our brains don't really have three distinct memory areas. Echoic memory, short-term memory, and long-term memory are more likely integrated elements of one single, highly complex memory system. The original three-system model of memory can be found at R. C. Atkinson and R. M. Shiffrin, " Human Memory: A Proposed System and Its Control Processes," in *The Psychology of Learning and Motivation,* vol. 2, ed. K. W. Spence and J. T. Spence (New York: Academic Press, 1968), 89–195.

9. A. Baddeley, *Human Memory: Theory and Practice* (Boston: Allyn and Bacon, 1998).

10. J. T. Wixted, "The Psychology and Neuroscience of Forgetting," *Annual Review of Psychology* 55 (2004): 235–69.

11. There are lots of books and articles about the neuroscience and cognitive psychology of proper names. One good place to start is C. Semenza, "The Neuropsychology of Proper Names," *Mind & Language* 24, no. 4 (2009): 347–69.

12. K. H. McWeeny, A. W. Young, D. C. Hay, and A. W. Ellis, "Putting Names to Faces," *British Journal of Psychology* 78, no. 2 (1987): 143.

13. B. L. Schwartz, *Tip-of-the-Tongue States: Phenomenology, Mechanism, and Lexical Retrieval* (Mahwah, NJ: Lawrence Erlbaum, 2002).

14. Cognitive psychologists call this *environmental context-dependent recall.* A recent article summarizing much of the research in this area is N. Unsworth, G. J. Spillers, and G. A. Brewer, "Dynamics of Context-dependent Recall: An Examination of Internal and External Context Change," *Journal of Memory and Language* 66, no. 1 (2012): 1–16.

15. Simply do a search on Amazon or Google for "remembering names" and you'll find dozens of books and websites describing these techniques in detail. Some of the most popular are H. Lorayne and J. Lucas, *The Memory Book: The Classic Guide to Improving Your Memory at Work, at School, and at Play* (New York: Random House, 2012); J. Foer, *Moonwalking with Einstein: The Art and Science of Remembering Everything* (New York: Penguin, 2011).

16. D. L. McCarty, "Investigation of a Visual Imagery Mnemonic Device for Acquiring Face–Name Associations," *Journal of Experimental Psychology: Human Learning and Memory* 6, no. 2 (1980): 145–55.

17. http://www.nlpco.com/library/interpersonal-relationships/remember-names/#axzz3NlL-9Trkh.

18. C. Semenza, "The Neuropsychology of Proper Names," *Mind & Language* 24, no. 4 (2009): 347–69.

19. L. E. James and D. M. Burke, "Phonological Priming Effects on Word Retrieval and Tip-of-the-Tongue Experiences in Young and Older Adults," *Journal of Experimental Psychology: Learning, Memory, and Cognition* 26, no. 66 (2000): 1378–91.

20. www.luminosity.com.

CHAPTER 7: ASKING QUESTIONS

1. There are several studies that show the benefits of asking questions and seeking help at work, including E. W. Morrison, "Newcomer Information Seeking: Exploring Types, Modes, Sources, and Outcomes," *Academy of Management Journal* 36, no. 3 (1993): 557–89;

J. S. Mueller and D. Kamdar, "Why Seeking Help from Teammates Is a Blessing and a Curse: A Theory of Help Seeking and Individual Creativity in Team Contexts," *Journal of Applied Psychology* 96, no. 2 (2011): 263; S. J. Ashford, "Feedback Seeking in Individual Adaptation: A Resource Perspective," *Academy of Management Journal* 29, no. 3 (1986): 465–87.

2. A. M. Ryan, L. Hicks, and C. Midgley, "Social Goals, Academic Goals, and Avoiding Seeking Help in the Classroom," *Journal of Early Adolescence* 17 (1997): 152–71.

3. T. J. Allen *Managing the Flow of Technology*. (Cambridge, MA: MIT Press, 1977), 194.

4. A good summary of how parents and teachers influence help-seeking behaviors in children can be found at R. S. Newman, "Social Influences on the Development of Children's Adaptive Help Seeking: The Role of Parents, Teachers, and Peers," *Developmental Review* 20, no. 3 (2000): 350–404.

5. Ryan, Hicks, and Midgley, "Social Goals, Academic Goals, and Avoiding Seeking Help in the Classroom."

6. Several studies have shown that males are often more reluctant to seek help, including F. Lee, "When the Going Gets Tough, Do the Tough Ask for Help? Help Seeking and Power Motivation in Organizations," *Organizational Behavior and Human Decision Processes* 72, no. 3 (1997): 336–63; M. E. Addis and J. R. Mahalik, "Men, Masculinity, and the Contexts of Help Seeking," *American Psychologist* 58, no. 1 (2003): 5–14.

7. You can read more about this fascinating study in F. J. Flynn and V. K. B. Lake "If You Need Help, Just Ask: Underestimating Compliance with Direct Requests for Help," *Journal of Personality and Social Psychology* 95, no. 1 (2008): 128–43.

8. This quote can be found in several places on the Internet, including http://thinkexist.com/quotation/he_who_asks_a_question_is_a_fool_for_five_minutes/164844.html . However, there seems to be some debate as to whether this is actually a Chinese proverb or who said it first.

9. D. Geller and P. A. Bamberger, "The Impact of Help Seeking on Individual Task Performance: The Moderating Effect of Help Seekers' Logics of Action," *Journal of Applied Psychology* 97, no. 2 (2012): 487–97.

CHAPTER 8: STARTING NEW RELATIONSHIPS

1. E. Berscheid, "The Greening of Relationship Science," *American Psychologist* 54, no. 4 (1999): 260.

2. More information about how the brain processes social rejection can be found at N. L. Eisenberger, M. D. Lieberman, and K. D. Williams, " Does Rejection Hurt? An fMRI Study of Social Exclusion," *Science* 302, no. 5643 (2003): 290–92. The benefits of acetaminophen for social "pain" is described in C. N. DeWall et al., "Acetaminophen Reduces Social Pain: Behavioral and Neural Evidence," *Psychological Science* 21, no. 7 (2010): 931–37.

3. Sociometer theory and the evolutionary reasons for our fear of social rejection are nicely described in M. R. Leary, "Affiliation, Acceptance and Belonging," in *Handbook of Social Psychology,* ed. S. T. Fiske, D. T. Gilbert, and L. Gardner, 864–97 (New York: John Wiley, 2010).

4. Leary, "Affiliation, Acceptance and Belonging."

5. K. Gonsalkorale and K. D. Williams, "The KKK Won't Let Me Play: Ostracism Even by a Despised Outgroup Hurts," *European Journal of Social Psychology* 37, no. 6 (2007): 1176–86.

6. Gonsalkorale and Williams, "The KKK Won't Let Me Play."

7. G. Downey and S. I. Feldman, "Implications of Rejection Sensitivity for Intimate Relationships," *Journal of Personality and Social Psychology* 70, no. 6 (1996): 1327–43.

8. E. Schiappa, M. Allen, and P. B. Gregg, "Parasocial Selationships and Television: A Meta-analysis of the Effects," in *Mass Media Effects Research: Advances through Meta-analysis,* ed. Raymond W. Preiss, Barbara Mae Gayle, Nancy Burrell, Mike Allen, and Jennings Bryant, 301–14 (Mahwah, NJ: Lawrence Erlbaum, 2007).

9. Leary, "Affiliation, Acceptance and Belonging."

10. These acquaintance expectations are described by famed sociologist Erving Goffman in his *Behavior in Public Places: Note on the Social Organization of Gatherings* (New York: Free Press, 1963).

11. My Babson colleague Wendy Murphy and her co-author Kathy Kram have written a wonderful book on how to develop supportive relationships at work, including mentors, coaches, and advisors. W. Murphy and K. Kram, *Strategic Relationships at Work: Creating Your Circle of Mentors, Sponsors, and Peers for Success in Business and Life* (New York: McGraw-Hill, 2014).

12. A. L. McGinnis, *The Friendship Factor: How to Get Closer to the People You Care For* (Minneapolis: Augsburg Books, 2004).

13. J. E. Dutton and E. D. Heaphy, "The Power of High-quality Connections," in *Positive Organizational Scholarship: Foundations of a New Discipline,* ed. K. Cameron, J. Dutton, and R. Quinn, vol. 3 (San Francisco: Berrett-Koehler, 2003), 263–78.

14. Dale Carnegie, *How to Win Friends and Influence People* (New York: Pocket Books, 1981).

15. N. L. Collins and L. C. Miller, "Self-disclosure and Liking: A Meta-analytic Review," *Psychological Bulletin* 116, no. 3 (1994): 457–75.

16. Social psychologists call this *spontaneous trait transference*, and you can learn more about it in J. J. Skowronski, D. E. Carlston, L. Mae, and M. T. Crawford, "Spontaneous Trait Transference: Communicators Take on the Qualities They Describe in Others," *Journal of Personality and Social Psychology* 74, no. 4 (1998): 837–48.

17. The concept of reciprocity in relationships is deftly described by my Babson and Stanford colleagues in A. R. Cohen and D. L. Bradford, "The Influence Model: Using Reciprocity and Exchange to Get What You Need," *Journal of Organizational Excellence* 25, no. 1 (2005): 57–80.

18. M. Goulston, *Just Listen: Discover the Secret to Getting Through to Absolutely Anyone* (New York: AMACOM, 2010), 59.

19. C. R. Colvin and D. Longueuil, "Eliciting Self-Disclosure: The Personality and Behavioral Correlates of the Opener Scale," *Journal of Research in Personality* 35, no. 2 (2001): 238–46.

CHAPTER 9: PERFORMING IN NEW SITUATIONS

1. "Evolution and Social Anxiety: The Role of Attraction, Social Competition, and Social Hierarchies, *Psychiatry Clinics of North America* 24, no. 4 (2001): 723–51.

2. Carol Dweck has published many articles describing the challenges with fixed mindsets, and summarizes much of her research in her best-selling book, *Mindset: The New Psychology of Success* (New York: Random House, 2006).

3. H. G. Halvorson, *Succeed: How We Can Reach Our Goals* (New York: Plume, 2010).

4. A general discussion of the impact of a fixed mindset on satisfaction, effort, and persistence can be found in Dweck, *Mindset*. It's also found in Halvorson, *Succeed*. The connection between a fixed mindset and academic performance can be found at L. S. Blackwell, K. H. Trzesniewski, and C. S. Dweck, "Implicit Theories of Intelligence Predict Achievement Across an Adolescent Transition: A Longitudinal Study and an Intervention," *Child Development* 78, no. 1 (2007): 246–63.

5. Once again, the unintentional impact of praise is described in Dweck, *Mindset*. Researchers have also found that overprotective, uncaring parenting is also associated with higher performance anxiety in children and college students; see G. D. Sideridis and K. Kafetsios, "Perceived Parental Bonding, Fear of Failure and Stress During Class Presentations," *International Journal of Behavioral Development* 32, no. 2 (2008): 119–30.

6. Blackwell, Trzesniewski, and Dweck, "Implicit Theories of Intelligence Predict Achievement."

7. L. J. Kray and M. P. Haselhuhn, "Implicit Negotiation Beliefs and Performance: Experimental and Longitudinal Evidence," *Journal of Personality and Social Psychology* 93, no. 1 (2007): 49–64.

8. A. W. Brooks, "Get Excited: Reappraising Pre-Performance Anxiety as Excitement," *Journal of Experimental Psychology* 143, no. 3 (2014): 1144.

9. These fears are described in D. Goleman, "For Stage Fright, Rehearsal Helps," *New York Times,* June 12, 1991, 2.

10. This advice comes from C. Arneson, "Performance Anxiety: A Twenty-first Century Perspective," *Journal of Singing* 66, no. 5 (2010): 537–46.

11. Do a quick search on Google and you'll find lots of information and advice on meditation and stress management. Some popular books on the subject include J. Kabat-Zinn, *Mindfulness for Beginners: Reclaiming the Present Moment--and Your Life* (Louisville, CO: Sounds True, 2011); and H. Gunaratana, *Mindfulness in Plain English* (New York: Simon and Schuster, 2011).

12. J. A. Mangels, B. Butterfield, J. Lamb, C. Good, and C. S. Dweck, "Why Do Beliefs About Intelligence Influence Learning Success? A Social Cognitive Neuroscience Model," *Social Cognitive and Affective Neuroscience* 1, no. 2 (2006): 75–86.

CHAPTER 10: GIVING BACK

1. Depending on the situation, we also need to ensure that newcomers have (1) equipment, resources, and training to perform their new role, (2) a challenging first assignment that helps them build relationships across the organization, and (3) a way to establish credibility and trust with other group members. There are lots of books out there giving comprehensive advice on how to onboard and train newcomers, especially new hires—for example, G. B. Bradt and M. Vonnegut, *Onboarding: How to Get Your New Employees Up to Speed in Half the Time* (New York: John Wiley, 2009); M. Stein and I. Christiansen, *Successful Onboarding: Strategies to Unlock Hidden Value Within Your Organization* (New York: McGraw-Hill, 2010).

2. For example, see E. W. Morrison, "Newcomer's Relationships: The Role of Social Network Ties During Socialization," *Academy of Management Journal* 45, no. 6 (2002): 1149–61.

3. For example, see T. N. Bauer et al., "Newcomer Adjustment During Organizational Socialization: A Meta-Analytic Review of Antecedents, Outcomes, and Methods," *Journal of Applied Psychology* 92, no. 3 (2007): 707–21.

4. D. W. Bray and A. Howard, "The At&T Longitudinal Studies of Manager," in *Longitudinal Studies of Adult Psychological Development*, ed. K. W. Schaie (New York: Guilford Press, 1983).

CHAPTER 11: GET OUT THERE AND SUCCEED

1. Social psychologists call this *hedonic adaptation*, and more information about this can be found at D. Kahneman, E. Diener, and N. Schwarz, *Well-being: Foundations of Hedonic Psychology* (New York: Russell Sage Foundation, 1999).

2. S. Lyubomirsky, K. M. Sheldon, and D. Schkade, "Pursuing Happiness: The Architecture of Sustainable Change," *Review of General Psychology* 9, no. 2 (2005): 111–45.

INDEX